GETTING READY
for MARRIAGE

GETTING READY
for MARRIAGE

10 SESSIONS

JERRY D. HARDIN & DIANNE C. SLOAN

THOMAS NELSON
Since 1798

Published in Nashville, Tennessee, by Thomas Nelson. Thomas Nelson is a registered trademark of HarperCollins Christian Publishing, Inc.

Thomas Nelson titles may be purchased in bulk for educational, business, fundraising, or sales promotional use. For information, please e-mail SpecialMarkets@ThomasNelson.com.

Scripture quotations are from the *New King James Version* of the Bible, © 1979, 1980, 1982, by Thomas Nelson. Used by permission. All rights reserved.

ISBN 978-0-7180-3497-9

Cover design: Studio Gearbox
Cover photo: © Stocksy Images
Interior Design: Kait Lamphere

First Printing August 2016 / Printed in the United States of America
HB 06.04.2024

To those who choose
to marry with love, knowledge,
and commitment.

CONTENTS

· · · · · · · · ·

FOREWORD

· · · · · · · · ·

a happily-ever-after ending.

When two people fall in love and decide to get married, they begin one of the most rewarding relationships God designed. Many couples believe the powerful feelings that motivated their decision to get married are enough to secure a healthy marriage. Yet sometimes, even during the courtship period, couples begin to discover that their feelings of love fluctuate and change. The only way to maintain true love and find that happily-ever-after marriage is to realize how many times love is not a feeling but a choice.

The decision to marry and maintain a monogamous, loving relationship requires understanding the dynamics of marriage and how your choices will affect your marriage. Couples will have much more fulfilling marriages when they begin to realize how many factors influence a happy marriage. These factors include family of origin, communication, conflict resolution, attitudes, religion, financial management, sexual relationship, and children. Each factor involves many issues that affect the well-being of any marriage. Each of the important factors that influence a marriage is examined in this workbook. Jerry and Dianne provide insight about how these areas will affect your marriage and provide worksheets to help you apply the information to your personal experience.

Let me take this time to congratulate you on your decision to marry. I also want to congratulate you for making such an important decision to prepare not just for the wedding ceremony but also for the marriage that will follow. *Getting Ready for Marriage* is one of the most thorough workbooks for couples preparing for marriage. You will benefit in years of a happy marriage from the time you spend using this workbook.

Frank Minirth (1947–2015)
Minirth-Meier Clinic

PREFACE

· · · · · · · · ·

Before the wedding is the time to talk about your expectations of marriage and the understanding you have of yourselves and each other in such areas as: family of origin, communication, conflict resolution, attitudes, religion, financial management, sexual relationships, and children.

Everything you bring into your marriage has been influenced by your family of origin. You are who you are because of what you have experienced, inherited, been taught, and seen modeled for you throughout your life. Your attitudes, morals, values, beliefs, and priorities are all influenced by your family and are the building blocks for the expectations you bring to your marriage relationship. Over the past fifty years, marriage counselors have come to understand that one of the most significant factors in a marriage is the influence of the family of origin.

Your family includes your father and mother, brothers and sisters, and all relatives, peers, friends, and others who have been significant in your life. All of these people have influenced you in what have become "your ways." Their influence has molded your perspective on life, and you probably see their way of relating as "the way" to conduct yourself in a relationship.

As you grow in your understanding of your beliefs, attitudes, expectations, values, and priorities, and those of your spouse-to-be, you can be more tolerant, patient, and loving in building a better marital relationship. By knowing more about yourselves and your families, and by developing better communication skills, you will become able to choose to incorporate into your marriage the good and healthy practices of each of your families and leave behind those ways that will hinder the growth of your new marriage. This is the first step in the creation of your new family.

As you work through this book, you can expect to make new discoveries about yourself and your spouse-to-be. You will learn how you are different from and similar to one another. Just remember that *different* doesn't mean "bad," nor does it mean "wrong." It just means "different." Don't expect to see everything the same way; that would be impossible. You come from different families with different sets of rights and wrongs—different ways of living life.

Good communication is the key that opens the door to a healthy, happy, and more stable marriage. Remember to share your differences openly and honestly, and begin seeking a solution to your problems.

This book is designed to help you expand your communication with one another and understand the commitment you are making when you marry. At the end of some sessions you will find a covenant. A covenant is a promise, a commitment. Like the covenant our Lord made with us, you will make a covenant with each other when you enter into marriage. The covenant you find at the end of some sessions is really just an expansion of the marriage vows. Make these covenants yours. Feel free to add to or adjust the statements as they apply to you and your spouse-to-be. If either of you has difficulty signing the covenants, it may be a sign that you need to talk more about the issues in that section or that you are just not ready to make a lifetime commitment.

While *Getting Ready for Marriage* is designed for you to work through together as a couple, we suggest you enlist the help of your pastor or a counselor for two reasons:

First, for accountability. As your wedding day draws near, a mountain of details will require your attention. It is easy to put off this important time for your relationship because, after all, you will be spending the rest of your lives together—right? Unfortunately, you probably won't take time for building your relationship after you marry if you don't make time now before you marry. Something will always be waiting to claim your time.

Second, you'll need help with the tough spots. When we encounter issues that are difficult for us to deal with, we have a tendency to think that love will take care of the problems for us, or it will be different after we get married, or we can change the other person. That usually doesn't happen. You have to deal with the tough issues, and it is better to deal with them before you get married rather than find out after you are married you cannot resolve the problems. Your pastor or a counselor can help you work on your communication skills as well as help you to step back from the issues you are working on to focus on finding the solution rather than focusing on just the problem.

ACKNOWLEDGMENTS

· · · · · · · · ·

would like to especially thank Dr. Dan Lord, our clinical supervisor, and the clinical family education/therapy staff: Dr. Dottie Schultz, Dr. Phil Stanberry, Dr. Bill Dorman, Professor Bill Allen, and Professor Mark Hicks, for the knowledge and wisdom you have shared with us.

We extend our thanks to the pastors and staff of Central Community Church, Wichita, Kansas, especially Senior Pastor Ray Cotton and Pastor Mark Deffenbacher, for their support of the Family Life Counseling Center. To the hundreds of couples who have participated in our Exploring Family Ties Workshops, we thank you for sharing your lives with us and for your critical evaluation of each section of this workbook.

And most importantly, we are grateful to Marilynn Hardin and Jim Sloan, our respective spouses for more than forty years, for their support, love, and interest in our lives.

Jerry D. Hardin
Dianne C. Sloan

LOVING YOU

· · · · · · · · ·

Love is one of the most meaningful, yet confusing, words in the English language. When spoken, shared, or received, love creates joy in the hearts of us all. Yet defining the word *love* or explaining it fully seems to be a task with which we all struggle.

Webster defines *love* as affection, an emotion, a sharing, a commitment — even as a definition of itself. We can love our God, our spouse, our car, our golf game, our friends; we can be in love or out of love. You and your spouse-to-be have experienced part of this entity called love or you would not be reading this book.

Because the English language has so many definitions for the one word *love,* we have distinguished three types: *emotional-love, friendship-love,* and *commitment-love.*

EMOTIONAL-LOVE

· · · · · · ·

*The feelings of "being in love," which at times
predominate over rational thought.*

· · · · · · ·

*Our feelings of love are conditional,
and feelings can change.*

For as long as humankind has existed, we have experienced emotional-love. We
have dreamed about it, talked about it, sung about it, written poetry to express it,
and, in recent years, acted it out in the movies and on television. Emotional-love,
or "being in love," can best be described as passion and is like no other feeling
we know. In fact, the feeling of being in love is probably what has brought you and
your spouse-to-be to engagement.

We communicate emotional-love through our senses: sight, smell, taste,
touch, and hearing. The couples we see in premarital counseling frequently hold
hands, kiss, and hug. They talk of music, words, and moments that belong only
to them. Their looks and touches send a clear message: "I am in love with you!"

Being in love is a God-given emotion that belongs in a marriage relationship,
but many couples consider this feeling of love as the *only* basis for their marriage.
The reality is that feelings come and go. Emotions can be lighted, like a fire. The
more you fan the fire, the more it grows. But a fire quickly flickers and goes out
if not attended. A fire needs fuel, care, attention, and air so it may breathe and
continue to burn. This feeling of love we have in our relationship also needs to be
cared for if it is to continue nourishing our relationship.

Many couples who have been married for some time tell us that their honeymoon is over—that the feeling of love has grown faint or has even left the relationship. They may have reached the point of saying, "I don't love you anymore!"
What they're really saying is, "I don't *feel loving* toward you any longer!" They
have not attended to their fire. This emotional love in a marriage relationship is
responsive. You must give to receive and receive to give.

Couples who consider being in love as the *only* basis for marriage will often
divorce when their emotions wane. They think they've lost their marriage because

they've lost their feelings for one another. A marriage based on feelings alone is destined to fail.

These feelings of love, which have attracted you and your spouse-to-be to one another and are helping you to begin bonding before marriage, are the special God-given joys of an intimate sexual relationship after marriage. An intimate sexual relationship within your marriage will fan the flame of your feelings and nourish your relationship. But sometimes problems come when couples engage in sexual intercourse before marriage. Stimulating the senses this way can heighten

can be sure "rational thinking" had very little to do

Remember your years as a teenager and young adult. Undoubtedly, you had times when you had strong feelings or attraction to another person. Some of those feelings could be called "puppy love," while others may have been more serious, but all were degrees of being in love. Would you have married all of those people? Of course not! Should you marry now based solely on those feelings? Of course not!

Take the time before you marry to be sure that the sweetheart you now choose will be your sweetheart after the next thirty years and more of marriage. You will need to separate your feelings of love from your thoughts about love. Your ability to make this separation is a key element of both friendship-love and commitment-love.

FRIENDSHIP-LOVE

. . . .

The intimate and affectionate support of one another.

. . . .

A friend is your needs answered and your life shared.

Friendship-love is the heartbeat of a happy, healthy, and well-functioning marriage. Within a marital relationship, each spouse should be able to grow and develop. As each spouse grows, your relationship will be strengthened. And as your relationship grows, so will you grow as an individual. Together, you create something new and become more than you can be alone.

A friendship is a nurturing relationship born when two people receive love from one another, and it grows and becomes stronger as each person gives to the other. As you give to and share with your friend, the bond between the two of you is strengthened. You can value the love of a friend above all things. When your spouse is your friend and companion for life, your marriage will be a blessing to you both.

Friends enjoy being together. Not only do you take time for your friends but you also make time for them. Everyone has 168 hours each week. How you use those hours says a lot about your values and priorities. You may tell me that you love me and say I am the most important part of your life, but if you spend every moment of your time on the golf course or with others, then I'll wonder how important I am to you.

Friends possess a mutual trust that allows them to be vulnerable with one another. You trust friends with more than your secrets—you trust them with your very life. With your friends, you share your hopes, dreams, joys, and victories, as well as your doubts, fears, sorrows, and failures.

Because you can trust a friend not to intentionally harm you, you can freely play together. You don't have to guard or protect yourself, so you can really be you. You can be spontaneous and relate without pretense. This freedom creates an environment for healthy communication.

A friend is your needs answered and your life shared. Here we see a joining of emotions and rational thinking. This friendship-love is a picture of reciprocity in its truest form. You choose to care because of what you learn about each other, what you share with each other; you choose to share your lives. You possess a mutual concern for the well-being of the other.

Friendship-love helps you love your spouse as your companion, someone with whom you will journey through life, someone to care for and someone who will care for you. As a friend and companion, you talk with your spouse, you listen to him or her, you take an interest in who your spouse is. You value your spouse's opinion and perspective.

COMMITMENT-LOVE

· · · · · · ·

A pledge binding one to another.

· · · · · · ·

*A covenant for the rest of your life, faithful and
permanent: that is commitment-love.*

God loves His people with a devotion that says, "I love you because you are you, not because of what you do or how I feel, but because of who you are." When you marry, you vow to love your spouse as God loves you, with commitment-love. You tell your mate, "I am here, and I'll always be here, faithful and permanent. You can count on me!"

Commitment-love establishes a covenant between two persons—a pledge binding one to the other—of everlasting certainty and stability. The difficulty of entering into this type of relationship is the same difficulty we have of entering into a relationship with God. To be in a covenant relationship, you must accept that you are no longer your own. You belong to someone, and someone belongs to you. We convey this in our wedding vows: "I take you to be my lawfully wedded wife/husband!"

Belonging in a marriage is created through commitment. We all need a sense of belonging, but not to the point of losing ourselves. An important task of marriage is to balance our need for togetherness with our need to retain our uniqueness. We become more than ourselves as we come together with our mates. But each of us still possesses our own unique self. There is now *you, me,* and *we.* In the eyes of God and the world, the "we" becomes a new creation in marriage.

The lighting of the unity candle in the marriage ceremony illustrates this new creation. Two lighted candles, representing the bride and the groom, stand at either side of a large unlighted candle. The bride and the groom each take a lighted candle and, together, light the center candle. The flames unite to create a new flame. The woman and man then return their candles, still lighted, to the stands. Three candles are now lighted. The woman and the man remain separate but, in marrying, have become one.

When you marry, you and your mate join together in a covenant relationship that cannot be separated any more than one of you could recover your part of the flame from the unity candle. This covenant leaves no room for the words, "I don't love you anymore!" Instead, you promise to love unconditionally; that is, you promise to give even if you don't receive. You make your husband or wife part of you and pledge to remain devoted to him or her.

A covenant for the rest of your life, faithful and permanent: that is commitment-love. Unchanging and God-like, it will preserve your marriage with certainty and stability.

Choosing to spend the rest of your life with someone is probably the most important decision you will ever make. You need to enter this covenant freely and willingly. If you feel trapped or coerced into making this commitment, resentment will build and your commitment will be difficult to keep. So *stop.* Look deep within your heart and answer the questions, "Am I ready to make a lifetime commitment to this person I am about to marry? Am I ready to commit to be wholly his or wholly hers, faithful and permanent?" If you answer yes—if you are ready to make a commitment founded on rational thinking, not just an emotional response to being in love—then your marriage will last.

SUMMARY

In your upcoming marriage, nothing is more important than to love and be loved and to understand what that means. Enter into marriage only if you are freely and willingly choosing to love your partner with commitment-love. With this God-like love, you covenant to devote your life to your spouse. You say, "You are wholly mine, and I am wholly yours!" You promise to always be there, faithful and perma- ... loving toward your mate. Commitment-love makes ... your spouse.

You value each other. You can trust your friend with your life.

Do you possess friendship-love for your partner? Can you and your spouse-to-be trust each other with your lives? If so, you are truly blessed with someone with whom you can journey through life.

The feelings of love that led you to become engaged will continue to be a special part of your relationship after the wedding. Emotional-love, or being in love, adds sweetness to your relationship. It is important to establish healthy patterns that will keep these feelings of love forever present; they must always be nurtured. Our feelings are sensitive and can change. The more you touch, hold, and kiss your mate—the more you stimulate the senses—the more often your feelings of love will be reborn.

Commitment, friendship, feelings are each a part of love, and each is necessary in marriage. Commitment-love will make a marriage last, friendship-love will make it strong, and emotional-love will make it sweet. All must be shared by you and the person with whom you are going to spend the rest of your life.

Do you love your spouse-to-be in all three of these ways? Does your spouse-to-be love you in all three of these ways? Now is the time to seriously look at the answers, because your life together depends on it.

KNOWING YOU

· · · · · · · · ·

With this pledge, you are making one of the most important commitments of your life. Do you really know this person you are about to marry? Does this person know you? Will your spouse-to-be be the kind of husband or wife you desire for a lifetime partner, and will you be the kind of husband or wife your spouse-to-be desires? What do you expect of each other? Will you get along, have fun, be happy, and work out your differences? What are your differences? Do you know? Questions! Questions! Questions!

If you are like most engaged people, these questions, along with others, are constantly racing through your mind. You are about to commit to spend a lifetime with this person, yet you may not have enough information to make a wise decision. You know you love each other. But you wonder if love is enough.

You have grown up in distinctly different families. You have your own thoughts and feelings about marriage, children, religion, sex, work and careers, and money management. Each of you has priorities and expectations about the way people should conduct themselves in a marriage. But have you openly discussed and evaluated your priorities and expectations? Unexpressed expectations are the seeds of trouble and conflict.

One of the first questions we ask couples in our premarital workshops is, "What do you think is the most important ingredient to have in a good marriage?"

The answers vary, yet each reflects what the men and women deem necessary to have a successful relationship.

What do you think is the most important ingredient to have in a good marriage? Without using the word *love*, write one word that best describes that quality.

_____   _____

Her answer   *His answer*

The word you wrote has significant meaning for your future marriage. Not only will you expect in your marriage the quality you described, you will require it for a happy, well-functioning relationship.

The worksheets in this book will help you review and evaluate the expectations you have of marriage, your priorities, and the relational patterns you have been taught or seen modeled for you in your families. When we conduct our premarital workshops, most couples tell us they would not have set aside, on their own, eight hours of intense, one-on-one sharing of their lives. But that is exactly what we are asking you to do with this book. Isn't the rest of your life that important to you?

As you begin knowing yourself and each other better, we want you to focus on three areas: *expectations*, *priorities*, and *behavioral patterns*.

EXPECTATIONS

· · · · · · ·

Eagerly awaiting the fulfillment of your needs and desires.

· · · · · · ·

Unexpressed expectations are the seeds of trouble and conflict.

You have expectations of married life. But are they realistic? You and your spouse-to-be grew up in different families with different priorities, behavioral patterns, and rules. Is it possible for either of you to fulfill the other's every expectation?

The source of many of the conflicts in the first years of marriage can be traced to one or both partners' expectations of marriage. Marriage counselors use the term *scripts* to identify these patterns of expectations. Your script tells how you believe the marriage should go, who should do what, and how it should be done. When your mate does not follow the script and meet your expectations, you experience disappointment, anger, and conflict.

People most often develop scripts, or form expectations of marriage, through an inductive thought process — that is, they reach the general conclusion of how marriage should be from a particular set of facts. Their set of facts comes from what they have observed in their family of origin and the knowledge they've

ship as partners become locked into their own ways of doing things. In marriage counseling, we frequently hear, "If I only knew then what I know now, I would never have married. This marriage is not at all what I expected." The question is, what did they expect? Clearly, one person had a specific notion of how the other should be or of how the marriage should go. One person's script was not followed.

Because you and your partner are working with different sets of facts, you probably will reach different conclusions about marriage using inductive thought. Both of you have sets of rights and wrongs from which you can develop distinct ideas of how marriages "should be." When faced with your differences, you will have to decide whose set of facts is right and whose picture of marriage is best. This can create considerable tension and competition.

Although most people use inductive thought, we have observed that couples in happy, healthy, well-functioning marriages approach their relationship with a deductive thought process. They decide what type of marriage they wish to have by looking at information about marriages from many sources and then choose what will work for them. These couples look beyond the marriages in their families to understand what makes for happy relationships. They read books to improve communication skills. They take time to attend classes and workshops that will help them in their relationship. They find their marriage can meet their expectations if they can discover the qualities that make marriages healthy, happy, and well-functioning and, together, find specific ways to incorporate those into their relationship.

Couples open to learning what makes a marriage work and willing to compromise because they value and respect the other's point of view will adjust to this relationship much better than those who approach marriage with a set marriage script. They agree to seek mutually acceptable ways of adjusting and adapting to the many challenges marriage presents.

The deductive thought process brings with it many new and exciting opportunities for growth and development. You and your spouse-to-be can find ample information about achieving a happy, healthy, and well-functioning marriage. You will learn what has worked for other couples and find that it may also work for you. When you incorporate into your relationship the good and healthy aspects of your two families, along with what you learn from the deductive thought process, you will receive the joys and blessings God intended for you.

PRIORITIES
. . . .

That which is superior in rank, privilege, or position.

. . . .

Your priorities in life give you direction and goals you think must
be achieved. They also indicate your loyalties to people.

What or who comes first in your life? This is an important question in every relationship. If you were to list the three most important people in your life, the three most important ways to spend your money after your marriage, and the three most important ways to spend your time, who and what would they be?

The important people in **her** life:

1. _____
2. _____
3. _____

The important people in **his** life:

1. _____
2. _____
3. _____

Her ways to spend money:

1. _____
2. _____
3. _____

His ways to spend money:

1. _____
2. _____
3. _____

Her ways to spend time:

1. _____
2. _____
3. _____

His ways to spend time:

1. _____
2. _____
3. _____

to the new family you will be creating with your spouse to be. This focus may be as difficult for you as it will be for your family. However, it is essential so you and your mate can develop your own family unit.

Your priorities also give you direction and goals you think you must achieve. Think of this direction as the path you have chosen to take you where you want to be. One of the important ingredients in a good marriage is a couple's sharing a common direction in life, a desire to travel the same path and achieve similar goals. Each of you will have interests of your own. But your priorities in relationships and how you want to spend your time and money reflect the character and values of you and your families, and these priorities need to be shared.

What comes first: a new home or a new car, higher education or a child, saving money or a vacation, your wife or your mother, your husband or your children? Where do you want to be five years from now? How about your spouse-to-be? Do you really want the same things out of life? Your priorities will change over the years as you grow and develop. And if you and your spouse communicate well, you will find your priorities growing, developing, and changing together. As you continue sharing and reevaluating your needs and wants, you will set new priorities, walk new paths together, and continue to go the same direction in life.

BEHAVIORAL PATTERNS

· · · · · · ·

The manner of conducting oneself.

· · · · · · ·

*Although behavioral patterns are passed down through
families, most patterns can be changed or improved.*

Behavioral patterns in relationships are more often caught than taught. Children tend to talk, walk, communicate, and treat people as their parents did. You probably relate the way you saw your family of origin relate. Unknowingly, you are following those same established patterns.

Behavioral patterns are passed down from generation to generation in healthy, well-functioning families as well as in unhealthy, poorly functioning families. Healthy patterns of intimacy, stable marriages, respect, honesty, and love of people, as well as unhealthy patterns of alcoholism, child abuse, divorce, and incest, show up in families through the years. Hugging, talking, and playing, or the lack of such activities, are also passed down from one generation to the next.

"She acts just like her mother," people say. Or, "He is a chip off the old block!" Aren't they the people you will most probably act like? Your mother and father have been your role models of how a man and woman should act toward one another for most of your lives.

You can gain insight and understanding of your script for husband-wife relationships and how individuals function in families by considering how the adults in your families interact, as well as how the parents and children relate. Are your parents close or distant? Do they hug, kiss, and show affection? Does your family play together, or is there someone who is never willing to play at all? Who is in charge and who sets the rules for the others to follow? As you step back and observe yourselves and your families, think of your family as a part of a multi-generational system. No one individual can do something good or bad without its affecting everyone else in the system.

Although these behavioral patterns are passed down through families, most patterns can be changed or improved. Patterns, like habits, can be broken or changed through awareness, knowledge, and choosing new behavior. That process of change begins through observation—identifying these patterns for yourself and your spouse-to-be—and continues with an open and honest sharing of thoughts and feelings.

During the first year of marriage you can establish healthy, nurturing behaviors that will set the many patterns for your relationship in the years to come. You will choose how you will behave toward one another. Even though your family of origin may not have shown affection, you can choose to show affection in your new family. Your new ways of relating may seem awkward at first, but as you practice and become more skilled, they will become a natural part of you. Remember,

important to be aware of the difference

you live it. Marriage is real life, not a dream or fantasy. Marriage brings with it real problems as well as real joys.

SUMMARY

You will never know everything about the person you have chosen to marry. But the more information you have before entering into this commitment, the less chance you will be confronted with unfulfillable expectations.

Everyone has expectations—for life, for work, and for relationships. The script you bring into a marriage is a map of your expectations for you and your spouse. If you want your expectations met, you have to let your partner know what they are—your spouse-to-be is not a mind reader. You need to communicate your expectations to each other and work together to fulfill them. Being open to learning new ways to make a marriage function well and working together to incorporate those into your marriage result in a happier relationship. Using the deductive thought process, you can consider all the good qualities, information, ideas, and experiences that have worked for others and make them a part of your marriage.

It is also important that you openly and honestly share those things most important to you—your priorities! What comes first in your life? What do you want to achieve and where are your loyalties? Priorities give you direction, and couples with common directions in life have more satisfying relationships than those who don't. As you grow together, your priorities will change. Good communication will help you negotiate those changes.

How you conduct yourselves in a relationship, and how you treat one another, will greatly affect your ability to work together to establish priorities and learn ways to fulfill your expectations of marriage. Families pass down behavioral patterns from generation to generation. You learn more from your parents' behavior than through any other teaching process, healthy and unhealthy patterns of how to treat one another, how to communicate, and how to solve problems. Children see, children do, and parents are the primary models for them. But as an adult, you have a choice about which patterns work for you and which ones you want to change.

Who is expected to do what in this new marriage? Is your family close or distant? Do they hug, kiss, and show affection, or is that simply not done? Examining the way you and your families relate will help you see the patterns you have inherited or learned.

In the following sections, the two of you will explore your expectations, priorities, and behavioral patterns, and those of your families, to begin to better understand each other. Complete only one session at a time. Give yourselves *at least* one hour to complete and discuss each session before moving on to the next. The important thing is to be open and honest with each other and not rush through the book.

Do you really know each other? Find out, as you get ready for marriage.

KNOWING YOUR FAMILIES

· · · · · · · · ·

for some families, the transition can be difficult. What changes in your relationship with your families have you noticed?

Your families may perceive your marriage as a loss. They may feel they have lost you to another family and things will never be the same. Or perhaps they see your marriage as your bringing another member into the family.

Take time to talk with each other and with your families about how your relationship with them is changing and how your relationship is changing them. What will you call your in-laws? Will you address them by their first names, or will they become "Mom" and "Dad"? How will you, as a new family, celebrate holidays? Where will you spend holidays and other special occasions? Will you eat two turkey dinners on Thanksgiving?

What are the special family rituals that everyone but your spouse-to-be knows? Are you expected every Sunday for family dinner? How do your families and you and your spouse-to-be feel about that?

Realizing that your marriage is creating changes in both of your families and talking with them about these can help to alleviate anxiety and prevent misunderstandings. It will help you understand patterns you may bring into your own relationship and also help both of your families begin to see you as a new, separate family.

EXPLORING YOUR FAMILY MAP TOGETHER

Creating a family map (genogram) will help you and your spouse-to-be get a better picture of your families. As you observe relational patterns in your families, try to see how they will affect your marriage. What are your relationships with your families of origin? Are your families close, where everyone is involved with each other's problems? Are you involved in many activities together, or do you see each other only on holidays and at weddings and funerals? Answering these questions will help you to anticipate your families' roles in the problems you and your spouse may encounter and expectations they may have of your participation in family activities after you marry.

A family map is a drawing of at least three generations of your family tree, which includes specific information about family members and their relationships. Family maps are frequently used by marriage and family therapists to help them observe and understand the history and patterns of their clients. You will be drawing your own family map to help you to take a step back and become an observer of your family.

Use the example of the family map (page 35) as you draw your own family map on page 38. The key to the symbols is shown on page 36. The more information you can record, the more you will learn about the behavioral patterns and history of each of your families. You may need to talk with family members to gather the information you need to complete your map.

As you and your spouse-to-be draw your diagrams, include the following:

- Names and dates of births (or ages), marriages, separations, divorces, illnesses, and deaths (including cause) for all family members.
- All miscarriages, stillbirths, foster, and adopted siblings.
- Occupation and education of family members.
- Serious medical, behavioral, or emotional problems; job problems, drug or alcohol problems; and problems with the law.

Are there others who lived with you or were important to your family? Add them off to the side of the family map.

What patterns of serious problems do you see? Write the ages or dates the problems began. How did your family handle the stress of job changes, health problems, and marriage and family problems?

Are there coincidences of dates for deaths, marriages, onset of illnesses, births? Did someone marry right after a family member died, for example? Or do any of these events typically fall around holidays? How do these events—deaths, marriages—influence you, your family of origin?

Include as much information as you possibly can. Your map doesn't have to be a work of art. Just be sure you can figure out who is in which family!

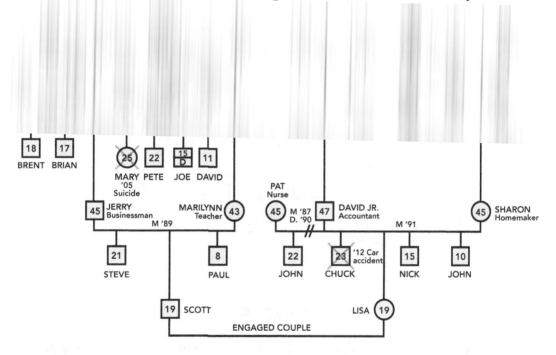

KEY TO THE FAMILY MAP

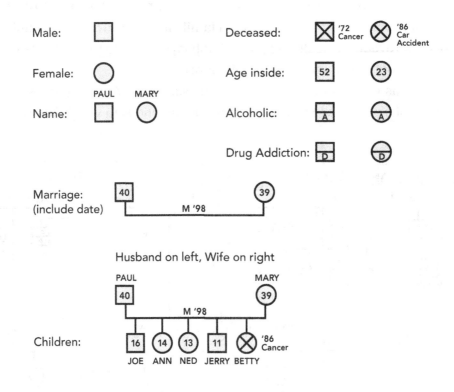

(GENOGRAM) SYMBOLS

Beginning with the oldest on the left, list each member of the family in the order of their birth. (Example: first child, son, 16 years old; second child, daughter, 14 years old; third child, daughter, 13 years old; fourth child, daughter, died age 2; fifth child, son, 11 years old.)

COMMON VARIATIONS

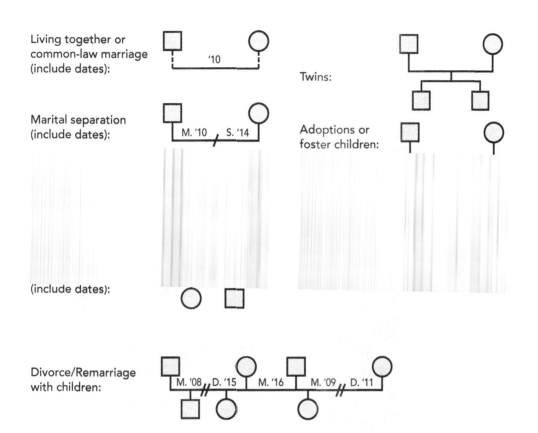

Living together or common-law marriage (include dates):   '10

Twins:

Marital separation (include dates):   M. '10   S. '14

Adoptions or foster children:

(include dates):

Divorce/Remarriage with children: M. '08   D. '15   M. '16   M. '09   D. '11

YOUR FAMILY MAP

Family patterns tend to repeat themselves. What happens in one generation will often happen again in the next generation. By being aware of the patterns of behavior in your families of origin, you and your spouse-to-be can make choices about the new family you are creating. Spend some time talking about the relationships in your families. With a red pencil, draw in the lines on your genogram for those who were:

Especially close

Distant

2. What kind of adjectives describes each parent? Brothers and sisters? You?
3. Where is the source of power in the family? How did others in the family deal with power/authority?
4. Who seems to energize your family? How?
5. Who are you most like? How?
6. Who are you most unlike? How?
7. What roles did/do family members have?
8. Do you see similar types of relationships in each generation?
9. What patterns of behavior would you like to see repeated or not repeated in the new family you and your spouse-to-be are creating?
10. Were you the oldest, middle, or youngest child? (What did it mean to be in a particular birth order in your family?) How will that affect your relationship?
11. Who are you closest to in your family? Why?
12. Who do you have the most conflict with? Why?
13. Are there any family secrets (*Uncle Joe drinks a lot; cousin Mary had a baby out of wedlock; Mom and Dad sleep in separate bedrooms*)? How did these secrets affect the family?

14. Who is religious in your families and who is not? List their religion or denomination. How did the practice of your faith affect your family?

15. Are there family members who have little to do with others in the family? What caused the separation? How does the separation affect the family?

16. Have there been marital separations, divorce, or remarriages in your families? How have family members managed these changes within the family? Are ex-spouses involved in family events, celebrations, and holidays? How are stepchildren included in the family?

As you can see by this process of exploring your family ties, the more you observe about your families of origin, the more you will understand your differences and similarities and their source. You are a product of the influences of your different families of origins, and when you marry, you marry families. Now that you have looked more closely at the patterns and relationships within your families, perhaps you have a better understanding of not only who you and your spouse-to-be really are but also what you can expect in the future.

Ask yourselves, *Is this the family I want to be tied to? Or are there too many problems? Do my future in-laws accept me? Does my family accept my spouse-to-be? What problem areas can I anticipate by looking at my family map?* These are valid questions, and talking with your spouse-to-be will help you find the answers.

COMMUNICATION

· · · · · · · · ·

Good communication is the art of sending and receiving a clear message. We are all continuously sending and receiving messages to and from one another. Even when we don't talk or write, we are sending a message that we want a separation from the other person. It is impossible not to communicate, but we can communicate poorly.

The art of good communication involves the sender, the receiver, and a clear message. How many times do we experience problems because we misinterpret the messages sent to us?

You and your spouse-to-be have each learned to communicate from your own families. You communicate differently because your families are different. For you and your spouse-to-be to enjoy life and grow together, you must be able to send the messages you mean and understand the messages you receive.

The most important factor in a good marriage is good communication. While finances, sex, or other issues may be the topic of heated discussions, marital dissatisfactions, and even breakups, *the inability of a couple to communicate and find a solution is the root of the problem.* So how can you and your partner communicate more effectively?

First, consider how you send a clear message. The words you use, the way you say them, and your body language add up to the total message you send someone. Communication experts have shown that only 7 percent of our message is sent from the words we say, 35 percent comes from our tone of voice, and the remaining 58 percent is sent through our body—eye contact, facial expressions, the shrug of our shoulders.

Many times one or more parts of our message differ—our words don't match our tone of voice or our body language, so the receiver of our message becomes confused. When confused, the receiver tends to hear the nonverbal communication above all other messages. Try this experiment with your spouse-to-be. Take one of your favorite phrases, such as "Boy, do I really love you!" Then say it to each other a few times, using a different tone of voice and body expression each time. Confusing? Probably. This happens frequently in our daily communication.

A clear message comes out of your being aware of what you are thinking and feeling and being able to share that information with your partner. This clear sharing of yourself leads to a happier, healthier relationship. Here are five key steps to better communication between you and your spouse-to-be.

FIVE STEPS TO BETTER COMMUNICATION

1. Take Time for One Another

In this busy world, you will find more and more areas of life demanding your time. It is not uncommon to make time or take time for less important commitments than sharing with the most important person in your life, your spouse-to-be.

You probably will spend more quality time sharing during your courtship than you will after your marriage. We frequently hear couples in marriage counseling say, "I am just being taken for granted." What they are really saying is, "I do not feel valued when you do not ask me what I think or how I feel." It is important to begin now setting aside a regular time for the two of you to listen to and share with one another.

2. Speak for Yourself

Be aware of your own thoughts and feelings and be responsible for communicating those to each other. No one can speak for you, except you! Use "I" messages: "I feel sad because"; "I think we need to take this approach because"; "I am really hurting right now"; "Let me tell you how I see this situation"; "This is how I feel."

Communication gets cloudy when you begin to tell your spouse-to-be what he thinks and feels or how she *should* think and feel. This frequently creates a defensive reaction from your partner if he or she perceives your interpretation

3. Understand That Your Partner's Perceptions Are Different from Yours

You will never see everything exactly the same way because you come from different families and different ways of life. *Different* does not mean "wrong"; it does not mean "bad"; it just means "different." Sometimes you may have to agree to disagree. You may have to say, "Well, I guess we really see that differently."

It is okay to see life differently at times. In fact, it would be unusual if you didn't. Good communication comes when you value and take the time to understand your differences. When you respect the perceptions of your spouse-to-be, you are saying, "Who you are and what you think is important to me." Couples who value one another will grow through teaching and learning from each other. Those who do not value the other's perceptions are saying, "You have nothing to teach me. My way is always right."

Poor communication is frequently the result of our trying to prove our rightness. Ask yourself if you would rather be right or be happy. Sometimes you can't have both. If you are *not* interested in hearing your spouse-to-be's point of view, you simply don't value what he or she thinks and feels.

4. Really Listen

Listen—not only to what is being said but also to the total message being sent. Remember, less than half of your message is communicated verbally, through words and tone of voice. It is important to listen to the nonverbal body messages as well, for those messages will frequently give you clues as to how your partner is *feeling.* At this stage in your relationship, you are probably very attuned to the nonverbal messages of your spouse-to-be. After you marry you will need to work at staying tuned in, for over time we have a tendency to begin assuming we know what our mates are thinking and feeling.

Take a step back and think about the ways you listen to one another. Most of us listen in three basic ways: *attentive listening, passive listening,* or *selective listening.*

Attentive listening is giving your full attention to someone. You not only listen to what is being said but also are aware of how it is said—the person's tone of voice and body. You are listening to the total message the other person is sending. You value what the other person is saying.

When you listen attentively, the stage is set for good communication to take place. You and your spouse are each given time to share fully your thoughts and feelings. You listen to the whole message instead of try to plan what you are going to say when it is your turn to speak. Attentive listening is one of the most difficult, yet necessary, elements of the communication process. It takes practice, patience, and respect for what your spouse-to-be has to say.

A *passive listener* may hear the words being spoken but not tune in to the rest of the message, and thus miss most of it! There is little value placed on what is being said or for the person who is speaking. When your attention is on the TV, the newspaper, texting, your cell phone, or other things, you are not able to communicate effectively. If your spouse-to-be or you are involved in another activity, it is not a good time to talk, and you will need to set a time aside when you both can devote yourselves to the discussion.

We are all, at times, *selective* in our *listening.* We hear only what we want to hear and filter out the rest. During courtship you are more apt to screen out unwanted words or information. You may put little or no importance on certain things being said and a great deal of value on other words or phrases.

Selective listening has a similar effect to putting blinders over your eyes. An interesting exercise in selective listening would be to ask five to ten people who had just listened to the same speech what the speaker said. Chances are each person heard the speaker a little differently. Each person may have tuned out those things that were difficult or painful to hear. This is selective listening.

If you find yourselves repeatedly struggling with one or both of you hearing only a portion of what the other person is saying, stop and take time to find the root of the selective listening. That will help you to begin to open up your communication process.

you can speak only for yourself. If you mind read, you a
partner! Checking out also lets the other person know you have been listening attentively and that you value him or her enough to make sure you understand what is being discussed.

Time, honesty, clarity, respect, value, and love for one another will help you and your spouse-to-be in the art of communication. Communication is a skill that can be learned and improved but it takes time.

Remember when you were learning to drive a car. You probably had a few jerky starts and stops or fumbles as you learned, and you really had to think about what you were doing. Learning to communicate in healthy, effective ways takes time, practice, and a lot of patience. Couples who have healthy, happy, well-functioning relationships have taken the time to develop good communication skills and use those skills every day. Do you value your spouse-to-be and what she has to say? Does he value your views? Do you take time to share your thoughts and feelings? What kind of listener are you: attentive, passive, selective, or a combination of all three? How would you presently rate your communication skills as a couple? Great? Average? Improvement needed?

The choice is yours, and the choice you make will affect the type of marriage you will have.

The statements on the "Her" Worksheets I and II and the "His" Worksheets I and II, pages 46–55, are about the communication process between each of you and your families. In the space designated with an asterisk on the worksheet for you, answer *T* for "true" to the statements that describe the most common situation for you. Answer *F* for "false" to the statements that describe a situation that is seldom true. Then, in the other space, respond the way you think your spouse-to-be would answer. Do your work alone, and then come together as a couple and discuss your answers.

Now . . . just relax and answer as quickly as you can after reading each statement. Your first response should be your answer.

"HER" WORKSHEET I

The hardest topic for my family to talk about is sex.	HIS ____ 1.	
	*HERS ____ 1.	
In my family when my parents were angry, they would hit or slap each other.	HIS ____ 2.	
	*HERS ____ 2.	
In my family I often heard the phrase "I love you" spoken among family members.	HIS ____ 3.	
	*HERS ____ 3.	
In my family each person's feelings were important, and we were encouraged to share and talk about them.	HIS ____ 4.	
	*HERS ____ 4.	
My father would often say one thing and do another.	HIS ____ 5.	
	*HERS ____ 5.	
In my family, yelling was one way of getting what we wanted.	HIS ____ 6.	
	*HERS ____ 6.	
My parents complimented their children openly.	HIS ____ 7.	
	*HERS ____ 7.	
There is a great deal of arguing and fighting in my family.	HIS ____ 8.	
	*HERS ____ 8.	
My parents listened to my opinion and tried to understand what I was saying.	HIS ____ 9.	
	*HERS ____ 9.	
My mother was the parent in charge of the family, and her word was law.	HIS ____ 10.	
	*HERS ____ 10.	

My father had to have the last word on everything.	HIS ____ 11. *HERS ____ 11.	
My parents went days without talking when they were mad at each other.	HIS ____ 12. *HERS ____ 12.	
In my family, everyone was encouraged to express his or her thoughts openly.	HIS ____ 13. *HERS ____ 13.	
When someone needed to talk to my father, he would stop what he was doing and listen.	HIS ____ 14. *HERS ____ 14.	
I often heard my father say to my mother, "You shouldn't feel that way."	HIS ____ 15. *HERS ____ 15.	

the door behind us.

My family enjoys playing together.	HIS ____ 19. *HERS ____ 19.
My mother frequently complimented my father.	HIS ____ 20. *HERS ____ 20.
My parents listened to each other's opinions.	HIS ____ 21. *HERS ____ 21.
In my family, it was okay to cry in front of each other.	HIS ____ 22. *HERS ____ 22.
I frequently saw my family kiss and make up after fights.	HIS ____ 23. *HERS ____ 23.
My father frequently complimented my mother.	HIS ____ 24. *HERS ____ 24.
My family did not keep secrets from one another.	HIS ____ 25. *HERS ____ 25.

You have completed the family statements. On pages 50–52, you will be answering statements concerning the communication between you and your spouse-to-be. Respond to the statements as you have in this set of worksheets, answering first for yourself and then as you think your spouse-to-be would answer.

"HIS" WORKSHEET I

The hardest topic for my family to talk about is sex.	*HIS _____ 1. HERS _____ 1.
In my family when my parents were angry, they would hit or slap each other.	*HIS _____ 2. HERS _____ 2.
In my family I often heard the phrase "I love you" spoken among family members.	*HIS _____ 3. HERS _____ 3.
In my family each person's feelings were important, and we were encouraged to share and talk about them.	*HIS _____ 4. HERS _____ 4.
My father would often say one thing and do another.	*HIS _____ 5. HERS _____ 5.
In my family, yelling was one way of getting what we wanted.	*HIS _____ 6. HERS _____ 6.
My parents complimented their children openly.	*HIS _____ 7. HERS _____ 7.
There is a great deal of arguing and fighting in my family.	*HIS _____ 8. HERS _____ 8.
My parents listened to my opinion and tried to understand what I was saying.	*HIS _____ 9. HERS _____ 9.
My mother was the parent in charge of the family, and her word was law.	*HIS _____ 10. HERS _____ 10.
My father had to have the last word on everything.	*HIS _____ 11. HERS _____ 11.
My parents went days without talking when they were mad at each other.	*HIS _____ 12. HERS _____ 12.
In my family, everyone was encouraged to express his or her thoughts openly.	*HIS _____ 13. HERS _____ 13.
When someone needed to talk to my father, he would stop what he was doing and listen.	*HIS _____ 14. HERS _____ 14.
I often heard my father say to my mother, "You shouldn't feel that way."	*HIS _____ 15. HERS _____ 15.
It is important in my family to respect the rights and privacy of each person.	*HIS _____ 16. HERS _____ 16.

In my family, honesty, above all things, was important.	*HIS _____ 17. HERS _____ 17.
My family primarily expressed anger by leaving the room and slamming the door behind us.	*HIS _____ 18. HERS _____ 18.
My family enjoys playing together.	*HIS _____ 19. HERS _____ 19.
My mother frequently complimented my father.	*HIS _____ 20. HERS _____ 20.
My parents listened to each other's opinions.	*HIS _____ 21. HERS _____ 21.
My family did not keep secrets from one another.	*HIS _____ 25. HERS _____ 25.

You have completed the family statements. On pages 53–55, you will be answering statements concerning the communication between you and your spouse-to-be. Respond to the statements as you have in this set of worksheets, answering first for yourself and then as you think your spouse-to-be would answer.

"HER" WORKSHEET II

It is very important to me that you accept my feelings.	HIS _____ 1. *HERS _____ 1.
I think we should be able to disagree without a fight.	HIS _____ 2. *HERS _____ 2.
Sometimes I am afraid to tell you what I really think.	HIS _____ 3. *HERS _____ 3.
I believe that arguing is very bad for a marriage.	HIS _____ 4. *HERS _____ 4.
I believe that both the man and the woman should be able to express their feelings.	HIS _____ 5. *HERS _____ 5.
I think I am an attentive listener.	HIS _____ 6. *HERS _____ 6.
I think that it is all right to talk about our married life with whomever I please.	HIS _____ 7. *HERS _____ 7.
Sometimes I need space before I can discuss something I am upset about.	HIS _____ 8. *HERS _____ 8.
I find it difficult to share my feelings.	HIS _____ 9. *HERS _____ 9.
When I have a problem, I believe you will be there to help me.	HIS _____ 10. *HERS _____ 10.
Loud yelling bothers me, and I withdraw when it occurs.	HIS _____ 11. *HERS _____ 11.
I find it difficult to criticize you without your getting angry.	HIS _____ 12. *HERS _____ 12.
It is important for me to show you how much I trust you.	HIS _____ 13. *HERS _____ 13.
Sometimes I need time to myself, and that doesn't mean I don't love you.	HIS _____ 14. *HERS _____ 14.
I am satisfied with my way of expressing anger.	HIS _____ 15. *HERS _____ 15.
I think we should be able to put each other down and make fun of each other.	HIS _____ 16. *HERS _____ 16.

It is important to me that you hug me at least once a day.	HIS ____ 17. *HERS ____ 17.
I believe you really care about my feelings.	HIS ____ 18. *HERS ____ 18.
The hardest topic for us to talk about is religion.	HIS ____ 19. *HERS ____ 19.
In our marriage I will communicate the message "I love you" by voice and action.	HIS ____ 20. *HERS ____ 20.
I think that you frequently talk down to me.	HIS ____ 21. *HERS ____ 21.
I try not to interrupt you when we talk.	HIS ____ 25. *HERS ____ 25.
In our marriage, I would like to have our serious talks just before bedtime.	HIS ____ 26. *HERS ____ 26.
Sometimes I can be very pushy and to the point.	HIS ____ 27. *HERS ____ 27.
Disagreement can be healthy in a marriage if both people fight fairly and resolve differences.	HIS ____ 28. *HERS ____ 28.
I think we both respect one another's thoughts and feelings.	HIS ____ 29. *HERS ____ 29.
You compliment me often when I do something well.	HIS ____ 30. *HERS ____ 30.
It is very important to me to know how you feel and what you think.	HIS ____ 31. *HERS ____ 31.
I am very sensitive to criticism.	HIS ____ 32. *HERS ____ 32.
I believe it is important to you to be right all the time.	HIS ____ 33. *HERS ____ 33.

I believe it is important to express our thoughts openly and honestly.	HIS ____ 34. *HERS ____ 34.
In our marriage, I don't think we should hit or call names.	HIS ____ 35. *HERS ____ 35.
I know I am very important to you.	HIS ____ 36. *HERS ____ 36.
When I get angry and you ask me what is wrong, I will often say, "Nothing."	HIS ____ 37. *HERS ____ 37.
I think the man should be the head of the house.	HIS ____ 38. *HERS ____ 38.
It is very hard for me to change my mind once I have made a decision.	HIS ____ 39. *HERS ____ 39.
I am satisfied with your way of expressing anger.	HIS ____ 40. *HERS ____ 40.
I believe it is okay to keep secrets from each other.	HIS ____ 41. *HERS ____ 41.
I feel close to you when you let me help you.	HIS ____ 42. *HERS ____ 42.
I would rate our ability to resolve differences as excellent.	HIS ____ 43. *HERS ____ 43.
Talking seriously is really hard for me to do.	HIS ____ 44. *HERS ____ 44.
I believe you really value what I am saying and try to understand.	HIS ____ 45. *HERS ____ 45.
I don't like you to touch me when I am angry with you.	HIS ____ 46. *HERS ____ 46.
I think you often interrupt me and try to dominate the conversation.	HIS ____ 47. *HERS ____ 47.
I think I am a difficult person to talk to.	HIS ____ 48. *HERS ____ 48.
I believe that if you don't get your way, you'll be angry with me.	HIS ____ 49. *HERS ____ 49.
I value your opinion.	HIS ____ 50. *HERS ____ 50.

You have completed the couple statements.

"HIS" WORKSHEET II

It is very important to me that you accept my feelings.	*HIS _____ 1. HERS _____ 1.
I think we should be able to disagree without a fight.	*HIS _____ 2. HERS _____ 2.
Sometimes I am afraid to tell you what I really think.	*HIS _____ 3. HERS _____ 3.
I believe that arguing is very bad for a marriage.	*HIS _____ 4. HERS _____ 4.
please.	
Sometimes I need space before I can discuss something I am upset about.	*HIS _____ 8. HERS _____ 8.
I find it difficult to share my feelings.	*HIS _____ 9. HERS _____ 9.
When I have a problem, I believe you will be there to help me.	*HIS _____ 10. HERS _____ 10.
Loud yelling bothers me, and I withdraw when it occurs.	*HIS _____ 11. HERS _____ 11.
I find it difficult to criticize you without your getting angry.	*HIS _____ 12. HERS _____ 12.
It is important for me to show you how much I trust you.	*HIS _____ 13. HERS _____ 13.
Sometimes I need time to myself, and that doesn't mean I don't love you.	*HIS _____ 14. HERS _____ 14.
I am satisfied with my way of expressing anger.	*HIS _____ 15. HERS _____ 15.
I think we should be able to put each other down and make fun of each other.	*HIS _____ 16. HERS _____ 16.

It is important to me that you hug me at least once a day.	*HIS ____	17.
	HERS ____	17.
I believe you really care about my feelings.	*HIS ____	18.
	HERS ____	18.
The hardest topic for us to talk about is religion.	*HIS ____	19.
	HERS ____	19.
In our marriage I will communicate the message "I love you" by voice and action.	*HIS ____	20.
	HERS ____	20.
I think that you frequently talk down to me.	*HIS ____	21.
	HERS ____	21.
I believe it is all right to call each other bad names when we argue.	*HIS ____	22.
	HERS ____	22.
I think that you have been open and honest with me.	*HIS ____	23.
	HERS ____	23.
I am willing to compromise to keep peace in our relationship.	*HIS ____	24.
	HERS ____	24.
I try not to interrupt you when we talk.	*HIS ____	25.
	HERS ____	25.
In our marriage, I would like to have our serious talks just before bedtime.	*HIS ____	26.
	HERS ____	26.
Sometimes I can be very pushy and to the point.	*HIS ____	27.
	HERS ____	27.
Disagreement can be healthy in a marriage if both people fight fairly and resolve differences.	*HIS ____	28.
	HERS ____	28.
I think we both respect one another's thoughts and feelings.	*HIS ____	29.
	HERS ____	29.
You compliment me often when I do something well.	*HIS ____	30.
	HERS ____	30.
It is very important to me to know how you feel and what you think.	*HIS ____	31.
	HERS ____	31.
I am very sensitive to criticism.	*HIS ____	32.
	HERS ____	32.
I believe it is important to you to be right all the time.	*HIS ____	33.
	HERS ____	33.

I believe it is important to express our thoughts openly and honestly.	*HIS ____ 34.	HERS ____ 34.
In our marriage, I don't think we should hit or call names.	*HIS ____ 35.	HERS ____ 35.
I know I am very important to you.	*HIS ____ 36.	HERS ____ 36.
When I get angry and you ask me what is wrong, I will often say, "Nothing."	*HIS ____ 37.	HERS ____ 37.
I think the man should be the head of the house.	*HIS ____ 38.	HERS ____ 38.
I feel close to you when you let me help you.	HIS ____ 42.	HERS ____ 42.
I would rate our ability to resolve differences as excellent.	*HIS ____ 43.	HERS ____ 43.
Talking seriously is really hard for me to do.	*HIS ____ 44.	HERS ____ 44.
I believe you really value what I am saying and try to understand.	*HIS ____ 45.	HERS ____ 45.
I don't like you to touch me when I am angry with you.	*HIS ____ 46.	HERS ____ 46.
I think you often interrupt me and try to dominate the conversation.	*HIS ____ 47.	HERS ____ 47.
I think I am a difficult person to talk to.	*HIS ____ 48.	HERS ____ 48.
I believe that if you don't get your way, you'll be angry with me.	*HIS ____ 49.	HERS ____ 49.
I value your opinion.	*HIS ____ 50.	HERS ____ 50.

You have completed the couple statements.

COMMUNICATION AND PERCEPTION EVALUATION

1. To evaluate the family communication section, compare your answers in both the "His" and "Hers" spaces from Worksheet I and give yourselves one point for each answer that is the same. There is a total of fifty points, two points for each statement. This is your communication and perception score for your families.

Family Communication and Perception Score _____

2. To evaluate the couple communication section, compare your answers in both the "His" and "Hers" spaces from Worksheet II and give yourselves one point for each answer that is the same. There is a total of one hundred points, two points for each statement. This is your communication and perception score as a couple.

Couple Communication and Perception Score _____

Total Family and Couple Communication and Perception Score _____

125–150   A score between 125 and 150 indicates that you have good communication and in many areas your perceptions are the same.

100–124   A score between 100 and 124 indicates that you may not have spent enough time together sharing your thoughts and feelings about yourselves and your families. Be open and honest with one another in these areas and set aside more time for serious talks.

0–99   If your score falls below 100, you have much to learn about each other and your families. Communication is the key to a good relationship. You must begin sharing your thoughts and feelings in order to know how you agree and disagree.

In this evaluation, you have established the level of communication and the perception of communication you have in your relationship.

PROBLEM AREAS EVALUATION

To evaluate your problem areas or those areas requiring more attention, compare your answers in the following manner:

1. Take only the answers from the "*His" space on "His" Worksheet II and compare them to the answers from the "*Hers" space on "Her" Worksheet II. These are your answers about yourselves.

discuss further but you are similar in most ways. Remember to seek a solution to your differences.

0–39   A score of less than 40 indicates that your backgrounds, your values, and your beliefs may not be compatible. You need to take more time to talk and, perhaps, to see a counselor before going on with marriage plans. Problem areas that are present before marriage will not just magically disappear after marriage.

Do not consider Worksheet I in the evaluation of problem areas for you as a couple.

HERS: HOW DO WE COMMUNICATE?

Using the five key steps for communication, describe the weaknesses and the strengths you see in how you and your spouse-to-be communicate.

My strength is: _____

My weakness is: _____

Your strength is: _____

Your weakness is: _____

Describe the area that you see as a strength in your relationship.

Describe the area that you see as the greatest problem area in your relationship.

Describe the area in which you feel *you need* the most guidance to have a better marriage.

Describe the area in which you feel *your spouse-to-be needs* the most guidance to have a better marriage.

HIS: HOW DO WE COMMUNICATE?

Using the five key steps for communication, describe the weaknesses and the strengths you see in how you and your spouse-to-be communicate.

My strength is: _____

My weakness is: _____

Your strength is: _____

Describe the area that you see as the greatest problem area in your relationship.

Describe the area in which you feel *you need* the most guidance to have a better marriage.

Describe the area in which you feel *your spouse-to-be needs* the most guidance to have a better marriage.

COMMUNICATION COVENANT

Marriage is a special kind of relationship. It is a covenant to be open, honest, and faithful, and it is permanent. Place your initials in the space following the responsibilities you agree to assume in the Communication Covenant. You have the freedom to make any changes to fit your personal relationship.

I understand that communication is the key to a successful marriage, so I agree to the following responsibilities:

1.	I understand that communication is the key to understanding and agree to be as clear and open as possible.		
2.	I agree to find a special sharing time each day to give my spouse my undivided attention.		
3.	When there is something important to discuss, I agree to turn off the TV and cell phones, turn off the outside distractions, and turn my attention to my mate.		
4.	I agree to share my thoughts openly and honestly with my spouse and give him/her my approval to share openly and honestly with me.		
5.	I agree to share my feelings openly and honestly with my marriage partner, and give him/her my approval to share openly and honestly with me.		
6.	I agree to be an attentive listener.		
7.	I agree never to call names, hit, or say "I don't love you" to my marriage partner.		
8.	I agree that it is okay to disagree about some things.		
9.	I agree to take responsibility for what I say and do.		
10.	I agree never to speak for you unless I first consult you.		
11.	I agree to be truthful with you.		
12.	I promise to hug you every day of your life.		
13.	I agree to spend time with you each year in activities that will enrich our marriage (e.g., taking a class together about marriage communication, attending a marriage retreat, taking several days to be by ourselves to focus on our relationship, reading and discussing material about marriage relationships).		

14. We have identified some statements about communication that we
    should take more time to discuss. I agree to set aside time to discuss
    with you the following:

    • _____

    • _____

    • _____

    • _____

    • _____

15. I agree that if, for any reason, our communication seriously breaks
    down, I will go with you to get professional help.

want only the best for us in our marriage relationship.

His signature: _____

ATTITUDES

· · · · · · · · ·

your experiences in life. The environment in which you grew up has played a major role in the development of your attitude about life. And the more you know about one another and your families of origin, the more you will understand what makes you who you are and why you each see life the way you do.

Your attitude about life affects everything you think, feel, say, and do. If you see life as a playground, then you approach each day eager to join in the games. If you see life as a battleground, then each waking moment is a struggle and you must always be prepared to defend yourself.

How do you see life? How about your spouse-to-be? How does your attitude concerning work, play, and marriage fit in with the attitudes of your spouse-to-be? How are they similar? How are they different?

How do your attitudes affect the way you act or respond to each other? What roles will each of you have in this new relationship? What is absolutely unacceptable to you and your spouse-to-be?

What about your families? Do they believe there is a certain way men and women should be, act, and live?

Men, when you look at your spouse-to-be, what do you see? When she becomes your wife, what do you think her role should be? Do you see your wife-to-be as a housekeeper, a cook, the person responsible for the laundry and dish washing? If you think of her as a housekeeper, then we can tell you the house had better be clean! But if you see your wife as your sweetheart, your friend, a person to share your life with, then the cleanliness of the house will not be your primary focus.

Women, when you look at your spouse-to-be, what do you see? When he becomes your husband, how do you view his role? Do you see your husband-to-be as a provider, lawn keeper, the person responsible for the care, upkeep, and maintenance of the cars and house? If your attitude toward your husband is that he is to be a Mr. Fix-It, then we can tell you the automobile and the house better be in good working order. You probably will have a "honey-do" list for him most of the time. But if you see your husband as your lover, companion, and friend, it will not be a major event if something does not get done around the house.

Your attitude sets the stage for your life's journey. It plays a major role in shaping what your marriage relationship will become. If you greet your mate with love and a smile, you will find love and something to smile about in return. The attitude you choose, develop, and cultivate will determine how the events of your life affect you and will also affect the expectations you and your mate have of one another. When you *choose* to express yourself in a caring manner, express interest in your mate, you send a message of peace and harmony.

The first four minutes you spend with your mate in the morning and the last four minutes you spend with your mate in the evening set the stage for how the rest of your time together will go for that day. The way you greet and part from your mate plays an important role in the building of your relationship.

As husbands and wives come together at the end of the day, they frequently bring home their problems and troubles from work and the outside world. Give yourselves time to adjust from work to family; otherwise, you will transfer tension from job to home. Have a special four minutes of greeting when you walk through the door after work. Save any discussion of the problems and cares of the world until you have had fifteen to thirty minutes of rest.

Home should be a haven, a resting place, a place you look forward to going. These first four minutes will help you set the stage for keeping your relationship open for communication and understanding.

The following statements in the "Her" Worksheets I and II and the "His" Worksheets I and II, pages 65–74, will help you explore your attitudes and the attitudes of your families about marriage relationships. The more you know about each other and your families of origin, the more you will understand how you see life and your attitude about the roles each spouse should play.

In the space designated with an asterisk on the worksheet for you, answer *T* for "true" to the statements that describe the most common situation for you. Answer *F* for "false" to the statements that describe a situation that is seldom true. Then, in the other space, respond the way you think your spouse-to-be would answer. Do your work alone, and then come together as a couple and discuss your answers.

My parents would not allow any beer or alcohol in the house.	HIS ____ 2. *HERS ____ 2.	
My father had "his chair" and no one else sat there when he was home.	HIS ____ 3. *HERS ____ 3.	
In my family, we regularly showed affection by hugging or touching.	HIS ____ 4. *HERS ____ 4.	
In my family, holidays such as Christmas and Easter, and birthdays are a family affair.	HIS ____ 5. *HERS ____ 5.	
My parents put the needs of the children before their own.	HIS ____ 6. *HERS ____ 6.	
Being on time was important in my family.	HIS ____ 7. *HERS ____ 7.	
My parents thought it was okay for each spouse to have a separate night out.	HIS ____ 8. *HERS ____ 8.	
In my family, the house was kept neat, orderly, and clean.	HIS ____ 9. *HERS ____ 9.	
My parents did not believe it was important to attend the children's activities.	HIS ____ 10. *HERS ____ 10.	

My family saw the world as being unfair.	HIS _____ 11. *HERS _____ 11.
My father believed you should work hard and be loyal to your employer.	HIS _____ 12. *HERS _____ 12.
My parents believed everyone should be present at the evening meal.	HIS _____ 13. *HERS _____ 13.
My parents believed that the father was the head of the family.	HIS _____ 14. *HERS _____ 14.
In my family, it was common for friends and family to drop in without an invitation and be welcomed.	HIS _____ 15. *HERS _____ 15.
My family loves vacations and plans a yearly event.	HIS _____ 16. *HERS _____ 16.
My parents believed it was wrong to get drunk.	HIS _____ 17. *HERS _____ 17.
My mother preferred to stay home and raise the children.	HIS _____ 18. *HERS _____ 18.
My parents believed household tasks, such as washing dishes, dusting, and vacuuming, should be shared by all members in the family.	HIS _____ 19. *HERS _____ 19.
My family thought that church was necessary for a good family life.	HIS _____ 20. *HERS _____ 20.
My parents believed both mother and father should work outside the home.	HIS _____ 21. *HERS _____ 21.
In my family, Mom "waited on" all of us.	HIS _____ 22. *HERS _____ 22.
My father took pride in a well-kept yard and car.	HIS _____ 23. *HERS _____ 23.
My mother was pampered by my father.	HIS _____ 24. *HERS _____ 24.
In my family, divorce was out of the question.	HIS _____ 25. *HERS _____ 25.

You have completed the family statements. On pages 69–71, you will be answering statements concerning the communication between you and your spouse-to-be. Respond to the statements as you have in this set of worksheets, answering first for yourself and then as you think your spouse-to-be would answer.

"HIS" WORKSHEET I

My parents believed that children should be seen and not heard.	*HIS ____ 1. HERS ____ 1.
My parents would not allow any beer or alcohol in the house.	*HIS ____ 2. HERS ____ 2.
My father had "his chair" and no one else sat there when he was home.	*HIS ____ 3. HERS ____ 3.
In my family, we regularly showed affection by hugging or touching.	*HIS ____ 4. HERS ____ 4.
My parents thought it was okay for each spouse to have a separate night out.	*HIS ____ 8. HERS ____ 8.
In my family, the house was kept neat, orderly, and clean.	*HIS ____ 9. HERS ____ 9.
My parents did not believe it was important to attend the children's activities.	*HIS ____ 10. HERS ____ 10.
My family saw the world as being unfair.	*HIS ____ 11. HERS ____ 11.
My father believed you should work hard and be loyal to your employer.	*HIS ____ 12. HERS ____ 12.
My parents believed everyone should be present at the evening meal.	*HIS ____ 13. HERS ____ 13.
My parents believed that the father was the head of the family.	*HIS ____ 14. HERS ____ 14.
In my family, it was common for friends and family to drop in without an invitation and be welcomed.	*HIS ____ 15. HERS ____ 15.
My family loves vacations and plans a yearly event.	*HIS ____ 16. HERS ____ 16.

My parents believed it was wrong to get drunk.	*HIS ____	17.
	HERS ____	17.
My mother preferred to stay home and raise the children.	*HIS ____	18.
	HERS ____	18.
My parents believed household tasks, such as washing dishes, dusting, and vacuuming, should be shared by all members in the family.	*HIS ____	19.
	HERS ____	19.
My family thought that church was necessary for a good family life.	*HIS ____	20.
	HERS ____	20.
My parents believed both mother and father should work outside the home.	*HIS ____	21.
	HERS ____	21.
In my family, Mom "waited on" all of us.	*HIS ____	22.
	HERS ____	22.
My father took pride in a well-kept yard and car.	*HIS ____	23.
	HERS ____	23.
My mother was pampered by my father.	*HIS ____	24.
	HERS ____	24.
In my family, divorce was out of the question.	*HIS ____	25.
	HERS ____	25.

You have completed the family statements. On pages 72–74 you will be answering statements concerning the communication between you and your spouse-to-be. Respond to the statements as you have in this set of worksheets, answering first for yourself and then as you think your spouse-to-be would answer.

"HER" WORKSHEET II

I want my friends and family to feel free to come over anytime without an invitation.	HIS _____ 1. *HERS _____ 1.
I think women are more emotional than men.	HIS _____ 2. *HERS _____ 2.
I believe the man and woman should share equally in providing income for the family.	HIS _____ 3. *HERS _____ 3.
I think it is important for both of us to be present at our children's	HIS _____ 4. *HERS _____ 4.
and goodbye.	
I think it is okay to jump from job to job if you can make a little more money by doing it.	HIS _____ 8. *HERS _____ 8.
I want a night out with my friends at least once a week.	HIS _____ 9. *HERS _____ 9.
I think it is okay after marriage to see friends of the opposite sex in the evening.	HIS _____ 10. *HERS _____ 10.
I think grocery shopping is woman's work.	HIS _____ 11. *HERS _____ 11.
It really bothers me to be late or to leave at the last minute.	HIS _____ 12. *HERS _____ 12.
I like things clean, orderly, and in the right place.	HIS _____ 13. *HERS _____ 13.
My mother and father had a happy marriage.	HIS _____ 14. *HERS _____ 14.
I do not believe it is important for women to get a good education.	HIS _____ 15. *HERS _____ 15.
I think our family time should be without cell phones and social media.	HIS _____ 16. *HERS _____ 16.

I need to have private time on a regular basis.	HIS ____ 17. *HERS ____ 17.
I believe it is okay to have a few beers or a drink or two in the evening.	HIS ____ 18. *HERS ____ 18.
I believe that marriage is forever.	HIS ____ 19. *HERS ____ 19.
It is important to me to pursue my own career.	HIS ____ 20. *HERS ____ 20.
I believe that the woman's place is in the home.	HIS ____ 21. *HERS ____ 21.
In our marriage, I think we should each have agreed-upon household duties.	HIS ____ 22. *HERS ____ 22.
I believe it is okay for men and women to have a hobby or sport they can enjoy without their mates.	HIS ____ 23. *HERS ____ 23.
It is important to me that you pursue your own career.	HIS ____ 24. *HERS ____ 24.
I believe that it is wrong to get drunk.	HIS ____ 25. *HERS ____ 25.
I think it is all right to show affection in public.	HIS ____ 26. *HERS ____ 26.
I believe that life is unfair most of the time.	HIS ____ 27. *HERS ____ 27.
I want to be in close contact with my parents by calling or visiting every day.	HIS ____ 28. *HERS ____ 28.
I believe that alcohol/drug usage creates problems in a marriage.	HIS ____ 29. *HERS ____ 29.
Vacations together as a family are important.	HIS ____ 30. *HERS ____ 30.
After marriage, I want to go on vacations without my mate.	HIS ____ 31. *HERS ____ 31.
I prefer living spontaneously to having a definite schedule each day.	HIS ____ 32. *HERS ____ 32.
I prefer not to eat leftovers.	HIS ____ 33. *HERS ____ 33.

Birthdays and holidays are important to me.	HIS ____ 34. *HERS ____ 34.	
The wife should feel free to work after the children are in school all day.	HIS ____ 35. *HERS ____ 35.	
I am a risk taker.	HIS ____ 36. *HERS ____ 36.	
I want my mate to go to church with me.	HIS ____ 37. *HERS ____ 37.	
After marriage, I want to have vacations with our families of origin.	HIS ____ 38. *HERS ____ 38.	
I believe men have a greater desire for sex than women.	HIS ____ 42. *HERS ____ 42.	
I would be upset if meals were not served on time.	HIS ____ 43. *HERS ____ 43.	
I like doing housework (i.e., washing, ironing, vacuuming).	HIS ____ 44. *HERS ____ 44.	
I think I am an easy person to talk to.	HIS ____ 45. *HERS ____ 45.	
It would bother me if my mate made more money than I did.	HIS ____ 46. *HERS ____ 46.	
I think men should make more money than women.	HIS ____ 47. *HERS ____ 47.	
I don't believe women should travel alone.	HIS ____ 48. *HERS ____ 48.	
Big families are happier families.	HIS ____ 49. *HERS ____ 49.	
It is very important to me that we are financially successful.	HIS ____ 50. *HERS ____ 50.	

You have completed the couple statements.

"HIS" WORKSHEET II

I want my friends and family to feel free to come over anytime without an invitation.	*HIS ____ 1. HERS ____ 1.
I think women are more emotional than men.	*HIS ____ 2. HERS ____ 2.
I believe the man and woman should share equally in providing income for the family.	*HIS ____ 3. HERS ____ 3.
I think it is important for both of us to be present at our children's activities.	*HIS ____ 4. HERS ____ 4.
I would like to live close to my parents.	*HIS ____ 5. HERS ____ 5.
I believe that women are more family oriented than men.	*HIS ____ 6. HERS ____ 6.
I think husbands and wives should kiss good morning, good night, hello, and goodbye.	*HIS ____ 7. HERS ____ 7.
I think it is okay to jump from job to job if you can make a little more money by doing it.	*HIS ____ 8. HERS ____ 8.
I want a night out with my friends at least once a week.	*HIS ____ 9. HERS ____ 9.
I think it is okay after marriage to see friends of the opposite sex in the evening.	*HIS ____ 10. HERS ____ 10.
I think grocery shopping is woman's work.	*HIS ____ 11. HERS ____ 11.
It really bothers me to be late or to leave at the last minute.	*HIS ____ 12. HERS ____ 12.
I like things clean, orderly, and in the right place.	*HIS ____ 13. HERS ____ 13.
My mother and father had a happy marriage.	*HIS ____ 14. HERS ____ 14.
I do not believe it is important for women to get a good education.	*HIS ____ 15. HERS ____ 15.
I think our family time should be without cell phones and social media.	*HIS ____ 16. HERS ____ 16.

I need to have private time on a regular basis.	*HIS ____ 17. HERS ____ 17.
I believe it is okay to have a few beers or a drink or two in the evening.	*HIS ____ 18. HERS ____ 18.
I believe that marriage is forever.	*HIS ____ 19. HERS ____ 19.
It is important to me to pursue my own career.	*HIS ____ 20. HERS ____ 20.
I believe that the woman's place is in the home.	*HIS ____ 21. HERS ____ 21.
I believe that it is wrong to get drunk.	*HIS ____ 25. HERS ____ 25.
I think it is all right to show affection in public.	*HIS ____ 26. HERS ____ 26.
I believe that life is unfair most of the time.	*HIS ____ 27. HERS ____ 27.
I want to be in close contact with my parents by calling or visiting every day.	*HIS ____ 28. HERS ____ 28.
I believe that alcohol/drug usage creates problems in a marriage.	*HIS ____ 29. HERS ____ 29.
Vacations together as a family are important.	*HIS ____ 30. HERS ____ 30.
After marriage, I want to go on vacations without my mate.	*HIS ____ 31. HERS ____ 31.
I prefer living spontaneously to having a definite schedule each day.	*HIS ____ 32. HERS ____ 32.
I prefer not to eat leftovers.	*HIS ____ 33. HERS ____ 33.

Birthdays and holidays are important to me.	*HIS _____ 34. HERS _____ 34.
The wife should feel free to work after the children are in school all day.	*HIS _____ 35. HERS _____ 35.
I am a risk taker.	*HIS _____ 36. HERS _____ 36.
I want my mate to go to church with me.	*HIS _____ 37. HERS _____ 37.
After marriage, I want to have vacations with our families of origin.	*HIS _____ 38. HERS _____ 38.
I would be upset if I had to live in a home that was a mess all or most of the time.	*HIS _____ 39. HERS _____ 39.
Children should not talk back to their parents.	*HIS _____ 40. HERS _____ 40.
We should have separate checking accounts.	*HIS _____ 41. HERS _____ 41.
I believe men have a greater desire for sex than women.	*HIS _____ 42. HERS _____ 42.
I would be upset if meals were not served on time.	*HIS _____ 43. HERS _____ 43.
I like doing housework (i.e., washing, ironing, vacuuming).	*HIS _____ 44. HERS _____ 44.
I think I am an easy person to talk to.	*HIS _____ 45. HERS _____ 45.
It would bother me if my mate made more money than I did.	*HIS _____ 46. HERS _____ 46.
I think men should make more money than women.	*HIS _____ 47. HERS _____ 47.
I don't believe women should travel alone.	*HIS _____ 48. HERS _____ 48.
Big families are happier families.	*HIS _____ 49. HERS _____ 49.
It is very important to me that we are financially successful.	*HIS _____ 50. HERS _____ 50.

You have completed the couple statements.

ATTITUDES COMMUNICATION AND PERCEPTION EVALUATION

1. To evaluate the family attitudes section, compare your answers in both the "His" and "Hers" spaces from Worksheet I and give yourselves one point for each answer that is the same. There is a total of 50 points, two points for each statement. This is your communication and perception score for your families.

Family Communication and Perception Score _____

Couple Communication and Perception _____

Total Family and Couple Communication and Perception Score _____

125–150 A score between 125 and 150 indicates that you have good communication and in many areas your perceptions are the same.

100–124 A score between 100 and 124 indicates that you may not have spent enough time together sharing your thoughts and feelings about yourselves and your families. Be open and honest with one another in these areas and set aside more time for serious talks.

0–99 If your score falls below 100, you have much to learn about each other and your families. Communication is the key to a good relationship. You must begin sharing your thoughts and feelings in order to know how you agree and disagree.

In this evaluation, you have established the level of communication and perception you have in your relationship about attitudes.

PROBLEM AREAS EVALUATION

To evaluate your problem areas or those areas requiring more attention, compare your answers in the following manner:

1. Take only the answers from the "*His" space on "His" Worksheet II and compare them to the answers from the "*Hers" space on "Her" Worksheet II. These are your answers about yourselves.

2. Compare these answers and give yourselves one point for each answer that is the same. There is a total of 50 points. This is your couple problem area score.

Couple Problem Area Score _____

40–50   A score between 40 and 50 indicates that you have some areas to discuss further but you are similar in most ways. Remember to seek a solution to your differences.

0–39   A score of less than 40 indicates that your backgrounds, your values, and your beliefs may not be compatible. You need to take more time to talk and, perhaps, to see a counselor before going on with marriage plans. Problem areas that are present before marriage will not just magically disappear after marriage.

Do not consider Worksheet I in the evaluation of problem areas for you as a couple.

HERS: WHO DOES WHAT?

In this section, circle the letter on the left that represents the person(s) in your family who performed the task indicated when you were growing up. On the right, circle the letter representing who you expect will do the same task in your marriage. When you both have completed your sheets, compare your answers.

Key: Husband [H], Both [B], Wife [W], Neither [N]

In my **family**		In my **marriage**
6. H B W N	Decide which social activities the children...	
7. H B W N	Do the lawn work.	H B W N 7.
8. H B W N	Help the children with homework.	H B W N 8.
9. H B W N	Pay the bills.	H B W N 9.
10. H B W N	Repair household appliances.	H B W N 10.
11. H B W N	Discipline the children.	H B W N 11.
12. H B W N	Is the boss.	H B W N 12.
13. H B W N	Do the hugging in the family.	H B W N 13.
14. H B W N	Buy the cars.	H B W N 14.
15. H B W N	Decide which church to attend.	H B W N 15.
16. H B W N	Take out the trash.	H B W N 16.
17. H B W N	Make the beds.	H B W N 17.
18. H B W N	Take the children to the dentist or doctor.	H B W N 18.
19. H B W N	Choose a house for the family.	H B W N 19.
20. H B W N	Set up social activities.	H B W N 20.
21. H B W N	Do the ironing.	H B W N 21.

22. H B W N	Decide where the family will go on vacation.	H B W N	22.
23. H B W N	Buy gifts for extended family members on birthdays and holidays.	H B W N	23.
24. H B W N	Will work for the family income.	H B W N	24.
25. H B W N	Vacuum the house.	H B W N	25.
26. H B W N	Keep the cars in running order.	H B W N	26.
27. H B W N	Wash the car.	H B W N	27.
28. H B W N	Arrange the furniture in the home.	H B W N	28.
29. H B W N	Make a major purchase on credit.	H B W N	29.
30. H B W N	Shop for clothes for the family.	H B W N	30.
31. H B W N	Wash the dishes.	H B W N	31.
32. H B W N	Cook.	H B W N	32.
33. H B W N	Decide future moves due to job change.	H B W N	33.
34. H B W N	Bathe the children.	H B W N	34.
35. H B W N	Feed the children.	H B W N	35.
36. H B W N	Do the laundry.	H B W N	36.
37. H B W N	Go to the children's sports and school activities.	H B W N	37.
38. H B W N	Dress the children.	H B W N	38.
39. H B W N	Buy gifts for the children's birthdays and holidays.	H B W N	39.
40. H B W N	Choose what we do for entertainment.	H B W N	40.
H B W N	Others:	H B W N	

Now compare and discuss your answers.

HIS: WHO DOES WHAT?

In this section, circle the letter on the left that represents the person(s) in your family who performed the task indicated when you were growing up. On the right, circle the letter representing who you expect will do the same task in your marriage. When you both have completed your sheets, compare your answers.

Key: Husband [H], Both [B], Wife [W], Neither [N]

In my **family**		In my **marriage**
6. H B W N	Decide which social activities the children…	
7. H B W N	Do the lawn work.	H B W N 7.
8. H B W N	Help the children with homework.	H B W N 8.
9. H B W N	Pay the bills.	H B W N 9.
10. H B W N	Repair household appliances.	H B W N 10.
11. H B W N	Discipline the children.	H B W N 11.
12. H B W N	Is the boss.	H B W N 12.
13. H B W N	Do the hugging in the family.	H B W N 13.
14. H B W N	Buy the cars.	H B W N 14.
15. H B W N	Decide which church to attend.	H B W N 15.
16. H B W N	Take out the trash.	H B W N 16.
17. H B W N	Make the beds.	H B W N 17.
18. H B W N	Take the children to the dentist or doctor.	H B W N 18.
19. H B W N	Choose a house for the family.	H B W N 19.
20. H B W N	Set up social activities.	H B W N 20.
21. H B W N	Do the ironing.	H B W N 21.

22. H B W N	Decide where the family will go on vacation.	H B W N 22.
23. H B W N	Buy gifts for extended family members on birthdays and holidays.	H B W N 23.
24. H B W N	Will work for the family income.	H B W N 24.
25. H B W N	Vacuum the house.	H B W N 25.
26. H B W N	Keep the cars in running order.	H B W N 26.
27. H B W N	Wash the car.	H B W N 27.
28. H B W N	Arrange the furniture in the home.	H B W N 28.
29. H B W N	Make a major purchase on credit.	H B W N 29.
30. H B W N	Shop for clothes for the family.	H B W N 30.
31. H B W N	Wash the dishes.	H B W N 31.
32. H B W N	Cook.	H B W N 32.
33. H B W N	Decide future moves due to job change.	H B W N 33.
34. H B W N	Bathe the children.	H B W N 34.
35. H B W N	Feed the children.	H B W N 35.
36. H B W N	Do the laundry.	H B W N 36.
37. H B W N	Go to the children's sports and school activities.	H B W N 37.
38. H B W N	Dress the children.	H B W N 38.
39. H B W N	Buy gifts for the children's birthdays and holidays.	H B W N 39.
40. H B W N	Choose what we do for entertainment.	H B W N 40.
H B W N	Others:	H B W N

Now compare and discuss your answers.

RESOLVING CONFLICTS

· · · · · · · · ·

our conflicts and problems is

couples will, at times, come into conflict, and those couples who focus on seeking a solution to their problems will resolve their differences more quickly and move on. The inability to resolve conflict comes from the failure to focus on the solution rather than the distress caused by the problem itself.

Couples who are unable to resolve a conflict or problem in their marriage get stuck. When communication breaks down and the couple cannot get by their problem, the intimacy in their relationship suffers. They pull back from each other, become defensive, and cease to be vulnerable. Relationships do not function in healthy ways when there are unresolved conflicts.

As you and your spouse-to-be learn to resolve the conflicts in your marriage in healthy ways, you will experience the joys and happiness God intends for you.

WAYS WE HANDLE CONFLICT

Most of us handle conflict in one of four ways:

1. *Conquest*: Hang in there until I win. I must win!

2. *Surrender*: Unless I give in, this conflict will go on forever. Defeat at least brings peace!

3. *Withdrawal*: Pull back for now. This is not over yet, but if I let the dust settle, I can see better how to win. Step back, regroup, and then go for the throat!

4. *Resolution*: Find a way in which I can live with you, I can trust and respect you, and you can trust and respect me.

How do you usually handle the conflict in your life? What about your future mate? How do the methods you both use affect your relationship? The process you and your spouse-to-be use to handle a conflict plays an important role in your relationship.

It is normal, and even healthy, for there to be differences between family members. This is not a sign that you cannot be happy, just that you feel and think differently. It is just a sign that you are two normal, healthy individuals.

Take a look at the figure below. Without discussing this exercise, count the number of squares you see. Now, tell your spouse-to-be how many squares you counted. Are the numbers different? Probably! Each of you organizes information differently and sees things through different filters. This puzzle is not really any different from the multitude of problems you deal with together every day.

Look at the puzzle again. There are 30 squares. See if, together, you can find them.

Remember, the best way to seek a solution to your problems in marriage is by working together. If you and your spouse-to-be never have a conflict or problem, it may indicate that one or both of you are repressing your feelings or are afraid of stating your opinion. You may be refusing to be real and vulnerable with each other.

To disagree is normal! To resolve that disagreement because we love and care about the other person is a process that we must learn! We all have problems. But some of us have learned to be better problem solvers!

often considered a secondary emotion and is frequently supported by feelings of which we may not be aware. Emotional hurt, rejection, fear, sadness, frustration, and humiliation can underlie our anger responses to our spouse and create road-blocks in our ability to resolve conflict in our relationship. Until these underlying feelings are identified and put on the table, our relationship can get stuck.

Anger is experienced when:

- Needs are not met;
- Goals are blocked or not reached;
- Values are trampled;
- And, most of all, when the "self"—the feeling part, or the heart—is hurt or taken advantage of, especially by someone who is supposed to love or care about us.

Here we need to stop! We need to understand that when we reach the point of hurting the other person, resolving the conflict can never be reached. Reason, logic, seeing the problem clearly, and even wanting to solve the problem is not what we are dealing with now. What we are dealing with is the *hurt,* and that hurt has been caused by the personal degrading, putting down, or slandering of one another.

That is now the focus you are dealing with, not the conflict that needed to be resolved. Beware of ringing the bell that cannot be un-rung and pushing the buttons that you know will only hurt the other and will surely lead to unhappiness. In all of our counseling with couples, we find when these four things are present—*love, respect, kindness*, and *forgiveness*—the results lead to resolving conflicts and healthier and happier marriages.

WAYS WE HANDLE ANGER

We tend to handle anger in one of three ways:

1. *Venting:* Fighting back, exploding verbally or physically. This approach tends to intensify anger and usually ensures that changes will not occur in the relationship.
2. *Suppressing:* Avoiding the issues, seeking peace at any price, or just forgetting the problem. Unfortunately, suppressed anger frequently leads to a person's withdrawing from a relationship, health problems, or an eventual explosion of rage.
3. *Processing:* Dealing with anger constructively. (This is the best way to handle anger.) Acknowledge that you are, in fact, angry. Then find positive ways to release your anger: take a walk, exercise, talk it out, write. Do whatever works for you that does not destroy property or hurt someone else. Try to figure out what is causing your anger. And share your feelings with your mate when you are in control of yourself and can do so from an "I" position rather than a blaming, "you" stance.

Venting or suppressing anger is a real danger to any relationship! In marriage there are three things you must never do:

1. Never hit!
2. Never call names!
3. Never say, "I don't love you!"

These three behaviors accompany anger when it is vented or suppressed and can damage your relationship beyond repair. At the very least, any of these can leave your partner wondering if he or she can trust what you say and do.

The ability to resolve conflict requires a mixture of rational thinking and creativity. It requires your being able to step back from your problems so you can define them, explore options for how to resolve them, and decide on a solution.

resolving the conflict.

3. *Set aside time* to deal with the conflict. When emotions are out of control, take time to step back, calm down, think, and then come back together.

4. *Define* the problem or conflict.

5. *Identify* each person's understanding of the problem.

6. *Discover* areas of agreement and disagreement.

7. *Stay on the subject* that represents the immediate conflict.

8. *Explore options* of resolution.

9. *Focus on the solution,* not the problem. How the two of you solve this problem should be your major concern.

10. *Value the other person.* When you value the ideas and feelings of your partner, you value that person.

11. *Seek common goals.* Goals give your marriage relationship direction. You and your spouse-to-be need to work together in deciding what the goals for your marriage will be. You need to have common goals to build intimacy in your relationship and give you guidelines in problem solving.

12. *Allow for the needs of each partner to be met.* Need-attainment is basic for survival and growth. When needs are met, conflict can be resolved. Identify the needs each of you has that are not being met in the conflict.

13. *Close the issue.* When a conflict or problem has been satisfactorily

resolved, close the issue with a kiss or hug. This is very important. It is an active sign that you have made a decision you can both accept and you are ready to move on.

HERS: REASONS FOR CONFLICT

In the following exercise you will identify the reasons you think you and your spouse-to-be come into conflict. Place an *X* in the column that best indicates the amount of conflict you think each item creates in your relationship. Put an *0* in the column that best indicates how you think your spouse-to-be will respond.

Reason	Frequently	Sometimes	Seldom	Never
1. Money				
2. Borrowing/credit				
3. Sex				
4. Having children				
5. Raising children				
6. Religion				
7. Alcohol/drugs				
8. His family				
9. My family				
10. His friends				
11. My friends				
12. His night out				
13. My night out				
14. His career				
15. My career				
16. How we communicate				
17. His jealousy				
18. My jealousy				
19. Time spent together				

20. Time spent apart				
21. Entertainment				
22. How he treats me				
23. How I treat him				
24. How we will spend holidays				
25. Who's right				
26. Others:				

HIS: REASONS FOR CONFLICT

In the following exercise you will identify the reasons you think you and your spouse-to-be come into conflict. Place an *X* in the column that best indicates the amount of conflict you think each item creates in your relationship. Put an *0* in the column that best indicates how you think your spouse-to-be will respond.

Reason	Frequently	Sometimes	Seldom	Never
1. Money				
2. Borrowing/credit				
3. Sex				
4. Having children				
5. Raising children				
6. Religion				
7. Alcohol/drugs				
8. My family				
9. Her family				
10. My friends				
11. Her friends				
12. My night out				
13. Her night out				
14. My career				
15. Her career				
16. How we communicate				
17. My jealousy				
18. Her jealousy				
19. Time spent together				
20. Time spent apart				
21. Entertainment				
22. How I treat her				
23. How she treats me				

24. How we will spend holidays				
25. Who's right				
26. Others:				

Now review your answers. Do you agree on the reasons you come into conflict? Spend some time using the good communication skills and conflict resolution skills that you have learned to discuss these areas.

HERS: WAYS WE EXPRESS ANGER

In the following exercise place a checkmark (√) next to the phrases that appropriately describe the way you and your spouse-to-be express anger.

Ways of Expressing Anger	His	Hers
1. Yelling at the other person		
2. Threatening the other person		
3. Blaming the other person		
4. Calling the other person names		
5. Saying nothing is wrong		
6. Losing self-control (throwing/hitting things)		
7. Pouting		
8. Saying hurtful words		
9. Drinking		
10. Wanting to be alone		
11. Being silent		
12. Stomping around		
13. Crying		
14. Becoming physically violent		
15. Starting some physical exercise		
16. Walking away and leaving		
17. Cursing yourself		
18. Using foul language		
19. Asking your mate for time to cool off		
20. Calling your friends or parents to let off steam		
21. Eating		
22. Sleeping		
23. Others:		

Now compare your answers. Do you express your anger similarly? Differently? Do your answers for your spouse-to-be match his? How does the way you express anger affect your spouse-to-be? How does the way your spouse-to-be expresses anger affect you? Discuss some of the ways you can help each other effectively express your anger.

HIS: WAYS WE EXPRESS ANGER

In the following exercise place a checkmark (√) next to the phrases that appropriately describe the way you and your spouse-to-be express anger.

Ways of Expressing Anger	His	Hers
1. Yelling at the other person		
2. Threatening the other person		
3. Blaming the other person		
4. Calling the other person names		
5. Saying nothing is wrong		
6. Losing self-control (throwing/hitting things)		
7. Pouting		
8. Saying hurtful words		
9. Drinking		
10. Wanting to be alone		
11. Being silent		
12. Stomping around		
13. Crying		
14. Becoming physically violent		
15. Starting some physical exercise		
16. Walking away and leaving		
17. Cursing yourself		
18. Using foul language		
19. Asking your mate for time to cool off		
20. Calling your friends or parents to let off steam		
21. Eating		
22. Sleeping		
23. Others:		

Now compare your answers. Do you express your anger similarly? Differently? Do your answers for your spouse-to-be match hers? How does the way you express anger affect your spouse-to-be? How does the way your spouse-to-be expresses anger affect you? Discuss some of the ways you can help each other effectively express your anger.

CONFLICT RESOLUTION COVENANT

1.	I understand that we will differ on many things, and I agree to respect your opinions and feelings.		
2.	I agree to be open and honest with you about my thoughts and feelings.		
3.	I agree that when we fight, we will come to a resolution as soon as possible.		
4.	I agree never to hit.		
5.	I agree never to call names.		
6.	I agree never to say, "I don't love you."		
7.	I agree that from time to time I may hate the things you do, but I'll never hate you.		
8.	I agree to take responsibility for my words and actions.		

9. We have identified some statements about fighting fairly that we should take more time to discuss. I agree to set aside time to discuss with you the following: • _____ • _____ • _____ • _____ • _____		
10. I agree that if for any reason we come to a problem we cannot solve, a fight we cannot resolve, I will go with you to get professional help.		

I agree to this Conflict Resolution Covenant because I love and respect you and want only the best for us in our marriage relationship.

Her signature: _____

I agree to this Conflict Resolution Covenant because I love and respect you and want only the best for us in our marriage relationship.

His signature: _____

RELIGIOUS ORIENTATION

· · · · · · · · ·

In the Scriptures, Jesus spoke about how His relationship to His people is like a marriage. That relationship is special, a covenant; in fact, a oneness. This oneness, this compatibility, is achieved only when you share the same basic beliefs. These are the very foundation of your marriage relationship. From this foundation come the building blocks of how you conduct yourselves, your moral standards, values, and ethics.

How compatible are you and your spouse-to-be in your religious beliefs? How do you see God? Who is God? Is Jesus Christ your personal Savior? What does that mean to you and your spouse-to-be? Will you, as a couple, go to church? Which church? How often? How involved will you be in the church? And how about baptism? When do you believe a person should be baptized and how?

These are only a few questions that can be important issues in a Christian relationship. What about a relationship between a Christian and a non-Christian, two nonbelievers, or two people of different faiths? How will your basic differences in religious beliefs affect your relationship and the relationship with your families?

In our premarital workshops we meet many couples from different denominations of the Christian faith. Denominational teachings and doctrines can vary to such a degree that a couple's understanding of God and life, and thus their compatibility, are directly affected. And these doctrinal differences can involve their complete family systems.

Religion has a deeper family interconnection than any other topic we will discuss. Couples may be able to come to a mutual understanding about their differences in denominational or religious teaching and doctrines, *but what about their families?* Families with strong denominational or religious beliefs may find it difficult or even impossible to accept the interfaith or interdenominational marriage of their children. This is one of the clearest reasons for the saying, "When you marry, you marry families."

So as you and your spouse-to-be complete this session, we want you to explore your basic beliefs and religious orientation and ask yourselves, *How compatible are we in our religious beliefs and orientation?*

The following statements on the "Her" Worksheets I and II and the "His" Worksheets I and II, pages 97–106, concern the way you and your families communicate about religion. Respond to these statements the same way you have responded to the statements in the previous sessions. In the appropriate space on the worksheet for you, answer *T* for "true" to the statements that describe the most common situation for you. Answer *F* for "false" to the statements that describe a situation that is seldom true. Then, in the other space, respond the way you think your spouse-to-be would answer. Do your work alone, and then come together as a couple and discuss your answers.

Now ... just relax and answer as quickly as you can after reading each statement. Your first response should be your answer.

"HER" WORKSHEET I

My family is actively involved in teaching or leadership roles in the church.	HIS ____ 1. *HERS ____ 1.
My family believes that right after you accept Jesus Christ as Lord and Savior you should be baptized.	HIS ____ 2. *HERS ____ 2.
My parents prayed with us before we went to sleep at night.	HIS ____ 3. *HERS ____ 3.
My family prays only at mealtime.	HIS ____ 4.
My parents believe that children are a precious gift from God.	HIS ____ 8. *HERS ____ 8.
My family considers water baptism necessary for salvation.	HIS ____ 9. *HERS ____ 9.
My parents made me attend church whether I wanted to or not.	HIS ____ 10. *HERS ____ 10.
My parents believe that God loves and cares about everyone.	HIS ____ 11. *HERS ____ 11.
My family prays together at times other than at mealtime.	HIS ____ 12. *HERS ____ 12.
My parents attended Bible studies regularly.	HIS ____ 13. *HERS ____ 13.
My family tends to push their religious beliefs on others.	HIS ____ 14. *HERS ____ 14.
My parents are Christians. They have received Jesus Christ as their Lord and Savior.	HIS ____ 15. *HERS ____ 15.
It is very important to my parents that the family goes to church every Sunday.	HIS ____ 16. *HERS ____ 16.

My parents would not accept their children marrying someone of another religion.	HIS ____ 17. *HERS ____ 17.
My parents believe that Jesus Christ is the Son of God.	HIS ____ 18. *HERS ____ 18.
My parents believe there is a heaven and a hell.	HIS ____ 19. *HERS ____ 19.
My family believes that a person is baptized only when they are put completely underwater.	HIS ____ 20. *HERS ____ 20.
My parents have strong religious beliefs.	HIS ____ 21. *HERS ____ 21.
My parents believe that Jesus was born of a virgin.	HIS ____ 22. *HERS ____ 22.
My parents are not very religious.	HIS ____ 23. *HERS ____ 23.
My parents believe that you must speak in tongues to be a Christian.	HIS ____ 24. *HERS ____ 24.
My family believes that you should be baptized at birth and never again.	HIS ____ 25. *HERS ____ 25.

You have completed the family statements. On pages 101 – 103, you will answer statements concerning you and your spouse-to-be. Respond to the statements as you have in this set of worksheets, answering first for yourself and then as you think your spouse-to-be would answer.

"HIS" WORKSHEET I

My family is actively involved in teaching or leadership roles in the church.	*HIS ____ 1. HERS ____ 1.
My family believes that right after you accept Jesus Christ as Lord and Savior you should be baptized.	*HIS ____ 2. HERS ____ 2.
My parents prayed with us before we went to sleep at night.	*HIS ____ 3. HERS ____ 3.
My family prays only at mealtime.	*HIS ____ 4.
My parents believe that children are a precious gift from God.	*HIS ____ 8. HERS ____ 8.
My family considers water baptism necessary for salvation.	*HIS ____ 9. HERS ____ 9.
My parents made me attend church whether I wanted to or not.	*HIS ____ 10. HERS ____ 10.
My parents believe that God loves and cares about everyone.	*HIS ____ 11. HERS ____ 11.
My family prays together at times other than at mealtime.	*HIS ____ 12. HERS ____ 12.
My parents attended Bible studies regularly.	*HIS ____ 13. HERS ____ 13.
My family tends to push their religious beliefs on others.	*HIS ____ 14. HERS ____ 14.
My parents are Christians. They have received Jesus Christ as their Lord and Savior.	*HIS ____ 15. HERS ____ 15.
It is very important to my parents that the family goes to church every Sunday.	*HIS ____ 16. HERS ____ 16.

My parents would not accept their children marrying someone of another religion.	*HIS _____ 17. HERS _____ 17.
My parents believe that Jesus Christ is the Son of God.	*HIS _____ 18. HERS _____ 18.
My parents believe there is a heaven and a hell.	*HIS _____ 19. HERS _____ 19.
My family believes that a person is baptized only when they are put completely underwater.	*HIS _____ 20. HERS _____ 20.
My parents have strong religious beliefs.	*HIS _____ 21. HERS _____ 21.
My parents believe that Jesus was born of a virgin.	*HIS _____ 22. HERS _____ 22.
My parents are not very religious.	*HIS _____ 23. HERS _____ 23.
My parents believe that you must speak in tongues to be a Christian.	*HIS _____ 24. HERS _____ 24.
My family believes that you should be baptized at birth and never again.	*HIS _____ 25. HERS _____ 25.

You have completed the family statements. On pages 104–106, you will answer statements concerning you and your spouse-to-be. Respond to the statements as you have in this set of worksheets, answering first for yourself and then as you think your spouse-to-be would answer.

"HER" WORKSHEET II

I think it is important to be actively involved in the church.	HIS _____ 1. *HERS _____ 1.
It is important to me to go to church every Sunday.	HIS _____ 2. *HERS _____ 2.
I believe that only men should teach in the church.	HIS _____ 3. *HERS _____ 3.
I believe God intended marriage to be forever.	HIS _____ 4.
I believe that because God forgives us, we should be willing to forgive each other.	HIS _____ 8. *HERS _____ 8.
I believe that a close relationship with God will help us to be true to our marriage vows and to each other.	HIS _____ 9. *HERS _____ 9.
I believe Christmas is a religious celebration rather than a secular holiday.	HIS _____ 10. *HERS _____ 10.
I think it is important that a husband and wife pray together.	HIS _____ 11. *HERS _____ 11.
I think it is important for us to be involved together at the church.	HIS _____ 12. *HERS _____ 12.
I believe God is faithful and willing to forgive us if we repent.	HIS _____ 13. *HERS _____ 13.
I consider it very important to read the Bible.	HIS _____ 14. *HERS _____ 14.
I think it is important to understand each other's ideas about religion.	HIS _____ 15. *HERS _____ 15.
Meditation is an important way for me to tune in to God.	HIS _____ 16. *HERS _____ 16.

I believe that my spouse-to-be and I have the freedom in God's eyes to call off our marriage now if we have any doubts.	HIS ___ 17. *HERS ___ 17.	
I believe that marriage is a choice to live with someone for life.	HIS ___ 18. *HERS ___ 18.	
I think it is important for us to attend church together.	HIS ___ 19. *HERS ___ 19.	
I believe that there is life after death.	HIS ___ 20. *HERS ___ 20.	
I believe that two people of different faiths can love each other and successfully live together in a marriage.	HIS ___ 21. *HERS ___ 21.	
I believe that God created marriage for a man and a woman.	HIS ___ 22. *HERS ___ 22.	
I believe that our marriage will be a sacred covenant.	HIS ___ 23. *HERS ___ 23.	
I consider the acceptance of Jesus Christ as my Lord and Savior the one and only thing God really requires of me for salvation.	HIS ___ 24. *HERS ___ 24.	
Our kids are going to church no matter what they think.	HIS ___ 25. *HERS ___ 25.	
I believe the books of the Bible need to be taken in context, with awareness of the time in which they were written and by whom.	HIS ___ 26. *HERS ___ 26.	
I would encourage our children to attend church regularly.	HIS ___ 27. *HERS ___ 27.	
I believe that Jesus Christ is the Son of God.	HIS ___ 28. *HERS ___ 28.	
I believe there is a heaven and a hell.	HIS ___ 29. *HERS ___ 29.	
I do **not** believe all Christians speak in tongues.	HIS ___ 30. *HERS ___ 30.	
I believe in the physical resurrection of Jesus Christ.	HIS ___ 31. *HERS ___ 31.	
It is important to me that my spouse-to-be is a Christian.	HIS ___ 32. *HERS ___ 32.	
I really do not consider myself a very religious person.	HIS ___ 33. *HERS ___ 33.	

I think that a marriage that includes God is stronger.	HIS	____ 34.
	*HERS	____ 34.
I believe that if you are a good person, you will go to heaven.	HIS	____ 35.
	*HERS	____ 35.
I think my spouse-to-be and I are compatible in our religious beliefs.	HIS	____ 36.
	*HERS	____ 36.
I don't believe that I have to belong to a certain denomination to be a good Christian.	HIS	____ 37.
	*HERS	____ 37.
I do not think it is important that a man and a woman have similar	HIS	____ 38.
	*HERS	38.
Both of our families are pleased about our religious beliefs.	HIS	____ 42.
	*HERS	____ 42.
I think we should counsel with a pastor about our religious views before we marry.	HIS	____ 43.
	*HERS	____ 43.
I believe the Bible is true.	HIS	____ 44.
	*HERS	____ 44.
I believe that attending church together will help us have a closer relationship.	HIS	____ 45.
	*HERS	____ 45.
I believe that the husband should be the spiritual leader in the family.	HIS	____ 46.
	*HERS	____ 46.
I believe that marriage is a covenant relationship blessed by God.	HIS	____ 47.
	*HERS	____ 47.
I think it is all right if I go to church alone.	HIS	____ 48.
	*HERS	____ 48.
I think religion is an area we need to discuss more with our families.	HIS	____ 49.
	*HERS	____ 49.
I believe we should have a Bible in our home.	HIS	____ 50.
	*HERS	____ 50.

You have completed the couple statements.

"HIS" WORKSHEET II

I think it is important to be actively involved in the church.	*HIS ____ 1. HERS ____ 1.
It is important to me to go to church every Sunday.	*HIS ____ 2. HERS ____ 2.
I believe that only men should teach in the church.	*HIS ____ 3. HERS ____ 3.
I believe God intended marriage to be forever.	*HIS ____ 4. HERS ____ 4.
I am a Christian. I have received Jesus Christ as my Lord and Savior.	*HIS ____ 5. HERS ____ 5.
I believe that God knows our needs even before we ask.	*HIS ____ 6. HERS ____ 6.
I believe infants should be baptized.	*HIS ____ 7. HERS ____ 7.
I believe that because God forgives us, we should be willing to forgive each other.	*HIS ____ 8. HERS ____ 8.
I believe that a close relationship with God will help us to be true to our marriage vows and to each other.	*HIS ____ 9. HERS ____ 9.
I believe Christmas is a religious celebration rather than a secular holiday.	*HIS ____ 10. HERS ____ 10.
I think it is important that a husband and wife pray together.	*HIS ____ 11. HERS ____ 11.
I think it is important for us to be involved together at the church.	*HIS ____ 12. HERS ____ 12.
I believe God is faithful and willing to forgive us if we repent.	*HIS ____ 13. HERS ____ 13.
I consider it very important to read the Bible.	*HIS ____ 14. HERS ____ 14.
I think it is important to understand each other's ideas about religion.	*HIS ____ 15. HERS ____ 15.
Meditation is an important way for me to tune in to God.	*HIS ____ 16. HERS ____ 16.

I believe that my spouse-to-be and I have the freedom in God's eyes to call off our marriage now if we have any doubts.	*HIS _____ 17. HERS _____ 17.
I believe that marriage is a choice to live with someone for life.	*HIS _____ 18. HERS _____ 18.
I think it is important for us to attend church together.	*HIS _____ 19. HERS _____ 19.
I believe that there is life after death.	*HIS _____ 20. HERS _____ 20.
I believe that two people of different faiths can love each other and	*HIS _____ 21. HERS _____ 21.

and only thing God really requires of the to

Our kids are going to church no matter what they think.	*HIS _____ 25. HERS _____ 25.
I believe the books of the Bible need to be taken in context, with awareness of the time in which they were written and by whom.	*HIS _____ 26. HERS _____ 26.
I would encourage our children to attend church regularly.	*HIS _____ 27. HERS _____ 27.
I believe that Jesus Christ is the Son of God.	*HIS _____ 28. HERS _____ 28.
I believe there is a heaven and a hell.	*HIS _____ 29. HERS _____ 29.
I do **not** believe all Christians speak in tongues.	*HIS _____ 30. HERS _____ 30.
I believe in the physical resurrection of Jesus Christ.	*HIS _____ 31. HERS _____ 31.
It is important to me that my spouse-to-be is a Christian.	*HIS _____ 32. HERS _____ 32.
I really do not consider myself a very religious person.	*HIS _____ 33. HERS _____ 33.

I think that a marriage that includes God is stronger.	*HIS ____ 34. HERS ____ 34.
I believe that if you are a good person, you will go to heaven.	*HIS ____ 35. HERS ____ 35.
I think my spouse-to-be and I are compatible in our religious beliefs.	*HIS ____ 36. HERS ____ 36.
I don't believe that I have to belong to a certain denomination to be a good Christian.	*HIS ____ 37. HERS ____ 37.
I do not think it is important that a man and a woman have similar religious beliefs before marriage.	*HIS ____ 38. HERS ____ 38.
I believe that Jesus, God, and the Holy Spirit are coequal.	*HIS ____ 39. HERS ____ 39.
I find it difficult to talk to my spouse-to-be about religion.	*HIS ____ 40. HERS ____ 40.
I want to be married in a church.	*HIS ____ 41. HERS ____ 41.
Both of our families are pleased about our religious beliefs.	*HIS ____ 42. HERS ____ 42.
I think we should counsel with a pastor about our religious views before we marry.	*HIS ____ 43. HERS ____ 43.
I believe the Bible is true.	*HIS ____ 44. HERS ____ 44.
I believe that attending church together will help us have a closer relationship.	*HIS ____ 45. HERS ____ 45.
I believe that the husband should be the spiritual leader in the family.	*HIS ____ 46. HERS ____ 46.
I believe that marriage is a covenant relationship blessed by God.	*HIS ____ 47. HERS ____ 47.
I think it is all right if I go to church alone.	*HIS ____ 48. HERS ____ 48.
I think religion is an area we need to discuss more with our families.	*HIS ____ 49. HERS ____ 49.
I believe we should have a Bible in our home.	*HIS ____ 50. HERS ____ 50.

You have completed the couple statements.

RELIGIOUS ORIENTATION COMMUNICATION AND PERCEPTION EVALUATION

1. To evaluate the family religious orientation section, compare your answers in both the "His" and "Hers" spaces from Worksheet I and give yourselves one point for each answer that is the same. There is a total of 50 points, two points for each statement. This is your communication and perception score for your families.

as a couple.

Couple Communication and Perception Score _____

Total Family and Couple Communication and Perception Score _____

125–150 A score between 125 and 150 indicates that you have good communication and in many areas your perceptions are the same.

100–124 A score between 100 and 124 indicates that you may not have spent enough time together sharing your thoughts and feelings about yourselves and your families. Be open and honest with one another in these areas and set aside more time for serious talks.

0–99 If your score falls below 100, you have much to learn about each other and your families. Communication is the key to a good relationship. You must begin sharing your thoughts and feelings in order to know how you agree and disagree.

In this evaluation, you have established the level of communication and perception you have in your relationship about religious matters.

PROBLEM AREAS EVALUATION

To evaluate your problem areas or those areas requiring more attention, compare your answers in the following manner:

1. Take only the answers from the "*His" space on "His" Worksheet II and compare them to the answers from the "*Hers" space on "Her" Worksheet II. These are your answers about yourselves.

2. Compare these answers and give yourselves one point for each answer that is the same. There is a total of 50 points. This is your couple problem area score.

Couple Problem Area Score _____

40–50   A score between 40 and 50 indicates that you have some areas to discuss further but you are similar in most ways. Remember to seek a solution to your differences.

0–39   A score of less than 40 indicates that your backgrounds, your values, and your beliefs may not be compatible. You need to take more time to talk and, perhaps, to see a counselor before going on with marriage plans. Problem areas that are present before marriage will not just magically disappear after marriage.

Do not consider Worksheet I in the evaluation of problem areas for you as a couple.

HERS: EXPLORING YOUR FAITH

In the space under the Bible verses, write your understanding of what these Scriptures mean.

For God so loved the world that He gave His only begotten Son, that whoever believes in Him should not perish but have everlasting life (John 3:16).

For all have sinned and fall short of the glory of God (Romans 3:23).

gin of God (Ephes...

After you have completed your answers, compare and discuss your responses with your spouse-to-be.

HIS: EXPLORING YOUR FAITH

In the space under the Bible verses, write your understanding of what these Scriptures mean.

For God so loved the world that He gave His only begotten Son, that whoever believes in Him should not perish but have everlasting life (John 3:16).

For all have sinned and fall short of the glory of God (Romans 3:23).

If you confess with your mouth the Lord Jesus and believe in your heart that God has raised Him from the dead, you will be saved. For with the heart one believes unto righteousness, and with the mouth confession is made unto salvation (Romans 10:9–10).

For by grace you have been saved through faith, and that not of yourselves; it is the gift of God (Ephesians 2:8).

After you have completed your answers, compare and discuss your responses with your spouse-to-be.

RELIGIOUS ORIENTATION COVENANT

Place your initials in the space following the responsibilities you agree to assume in the Religious Orientation Covenant.

Marriage is a special kind of relationship. It is a covenant to be open, honest, **faithful, and permanent. In our religious beliefs we must both be clear about how we feel and what we think so we can increase our understanding of one another.**

1.	I agree that we may differ on many things, and I agree to respect your opinion and feelings.		
2.	I agree to be open and honest about my religious beliefs.		
3.	I agree to always be willing to let you share with me your thoughts and feelings.		
4.	I agree that human life is a gift from God and will never abuse it.		
5.	I agree that we are answerable to God for the way in which we live our married life.		
6.	I agree that when we say "yes" to each other on our wedding day, we take each other for life.		
7.	I agree to make our marriage relationship my highest priority because I love you.		
8.	We have identified some statements about religion that we should take more time to discuss. I agree to set aside time to discuss with you the following: • _____ • _____ • _____ • _____ • _____		
9.	I agree that if for any reason we come to a religious problem we cannot solve, I will go with you to get professional help.		

I agree to this Religious Orientation Covenant because I love and respect you and want only the best for us in our marriage relationship.

Her signature: _____

I agree to this Religious Orientation Covenant because I love and respect you and want only the best for us in our marriage relationship.

His signature: _____

MONEY MATTERS

· · · · · · · · ·

Money is simply a medium of exchange, but the use of it gets tangled up in emotional complexities: love, power, family relationships, and self-worth.

You may be surprised to learn that money matters cause the most conflict in a marriage relationship.

Your attitude about money comes from your religious teaching and your family of origin. The New Testament addresses the subject of money more frequently than any other subject except the kingdom of God. The scriptural messages on finances are very clear: We should love people and use things, not love things and use people. The Bible also teaches that we are to be good stewards of our money and make wise investments. We are not to treasure *things* more than relationships because our hearts will be where our treasure is. The greatest treasure you can have is your relationship with God and with your chosen mate.

From your families you learned how to communicate about the way money is to be used. Think about the conversations you may have had with your parents, or overheard your parents have, about money. Were there frequent arguments about purchases made? Were items purchased in secret? What happened when the budget was overspent?

Money—the love of it, how you earn it, and how you spend it—tells more about your priorities than almost any other area of your lives. When we begin discussing monetary issues, how clearly we all can see greed, selfishness, covetousness, as well as generosity, good stewardship, and wisdom in ourselves and those around us. It is estimated that the root cause of at least 75 to 80 percent of all divorces is clashes over money.

Like all other areas of your marriage relationship, it is essential that you communicate about your finances. How did your family of origin handle money? Was cash paid for everything, or did your family use credit cards? How do you feel about the use of credit? How much should be given to the church? What does your spouse-to-be think?

What part did God's teaching play in your family's use of money? What about the family of your spouse-to-be? Did they have a budget they followed? What did they value? What were their priorities? How was money spent? Who made the decisions concerning finances?

Money is simply a medium of exchange, but the use of it gets tangled up in emotional complexities: love, power, family relationships, and self-worth. For some people, controlling the money in the family means they have the power in the family. What does money mean to you, and what does it mean to the person you plan to marry?

As you and your spouse-to-be begin looking at your financial picture, you will need to know something about your individual ideas of needs and wants. Today, many of our wants have become translated into needs. What has become a necessity for you? Do you consider a television a luxury or a necessity? Is eating at fast-food restaurants five nights a week more important than eating at a nicer restaurant once a week?

Most of us have received very little training in managing money. But many of our financial problems can be avoided by being aware of several important biblical concepts of good money management.

1. Let God set the standard for the love and use of your money. Be aware of the ways in which money can be a threat to both your relationship with God and your mate.
2. A budget is a necessity. Establish a simple, flexible financial outline (budget) to help you and your spouse-to-be meet the goals and priorities you set together. Remember, this is a joint project!
3. Establish a simple method of record-keeping from the day you get married. "Uncle Sam" requires it.
4. Communicate. Along with knowing and feeling that you are working together toward common financial goals, communication is essential.

5. Establish early in your marriage how you will use credit and credit cards. Set limits. Avoid becoming "credit-card junkies."

6. Establish an emergency fund. And decide in advance what constitutes an emergency!

7. Make savings a "fixed item" in your budget.

8. Be open to changing your budget as your goals, priorities, and family change.

In the life of every marriage, the time comes when couples find themselves in a financial squeeze. Make a pledge today that when that time comes for you, you will set aside a quiet evening or afternoon to discuss the problem and decide on a plan of action to help you overcome it. Remember, it is your squeeze *as a couple*, not just you as an individual.

The following statements on the "Her" Worksheets I and II and the "His" Worksheets I and II, pages 116–125, are about your attitudes and the attitudes of your families concerning money matters. Respond *T* and *F* to these statements as you have in previous sessions.

"HER" WORKSHEET I

My family had clear goals of what they needed to buy.	HIS ____ 1. *HERS ____ 1.
My parents were extremely cautious about going into debt.	HIS ____ 2. *HERS ____ 2.
My parents frequently fought over how to spend their money.	HIS ____ 3. *HERS ____ 3.
In my family, it is understood that we are not expected to support our parents in their old age.	HIS ____ 4. *HERS ____ 4.
In my family, we seldom used the air conditioner at home so we could save money.	HIS ____ 5. *HERS ____ 5.
It was important in my family to save for future emergencies.	HIS ____ 6. *HERS ____ 6.
My family felt that making donations to church was important.	HIS ____ 7. *HERS ____ 7.
My family set aside special money for family vacations.	HIS ____ 8. *HERS ____ 8.
The male in my family was the primary provider.	HIS ____ 9. *HERS ____ 9.
There were money "secrets" in my family.	HIS ____ 10. *HERS ____ 10.
My family seemed to have financial difficulties frequently.	HIS ____ 11. *HERS ____ 11.
My father usually left a good tip for the waitress/waiter in restaurants.	HIS ____ 12. *HERS ____ 12.
My family worked out a budget to live on and followed it to the penny.	HIS ____ 13. *HERS ____ 13.
My parents spent a lot of time shopping for a good buy before making a decision.	HIS ____ 14. *HERS ____ 14.
My family considered God's teaching in their financial decisions.	HIS ____ 15. *HERS ____ 15.
My family has had financial problems as long as I can remember.	HIS ____ 16. *HERS ____ 16.

My parents were very careful in their use of credit cards.	HIS ____ 17. *HERS ____ 17.
We considered working more important than time with the family.	HIS ____ 18. *HERS ____ 18.
In my family, we used coupons.	HIS ____ 19. *HERS ____ 19.
My mother handled the household bills.	HIS ____ 20. *HERS ____ 20.
Gambling was not an acceptable use of money.	HIS ____ 21. *HERS ____ 21.
My father paid the bill when we went out to a restaurant or hotel.	HIS ____ 22. *HERS ____ 22.
Having the latest styles of clothing was very important to my family.	HIS ____ 23. *HERS ____ 23.
My family believed it was important to pay all the bills when they were due.	HIS ____ 24. *HERS ____ 24.
My mother would give us money and say, "Now, don't tell your father."	HIS ____ 25. *HERS ____ 25.

You have completed the family statements. On pages 120–122 you will answer statements concerning you and your spouse-to-be. Respond to the statements as you have in this set of worksheets, answering first for yourself and then as you think your spouse-to-be would answer.

"HIS" WORKSHEET I

My family had clear goals of what they needed to buy.	*HIS _____ 1. HERS _____ 1.
My parents were extremely cautious about going into debt.	*HIS _____ 2. HERS _____ 2.
My parents frequently fought over how to spend their money.	*HIS _____ 3. HERS _____ 3.
In my family, it is understood that we are not expected to support our parents in their old age.	*HIS _____ 4. HERS _____ 4.
In my family, we seldom used the air conditioner at home so we could save money.	*HIS _____ 5. HERS _____ 5.
It was important in my family to save for future emergencies.	*HIS _____ 6. HERS _____ 6.
My family felt that making donations to church was important.	*HIS _____ 7. HERS _____ 7.
My family set aside special money for family vacations.	*HIS _____ 8. HERS _____ 8.
The male in my family was the primary provider.	*HIS _____ 9. HERS _____ 9.
There were money "secrets" in my family.	*HIS _____ 10. HERS _____ 10.
My family seemed to have financial difficulties frequently.	*HIS _____ 11. HERS _____ 11.
My father usually left a good tip for the waitress/waiter in restaurants.	*HIS _____ 12. HERS _____ 12.
My family worked out a budget to live on and followed it to the penny.	*HIS _____ 13. HERS _____ 13.
My parents spent a lot of time shopping for a good buy before making a decision.	*HIS _____ 14. HERS _____ 14.
My family considered God's teaching in their financial decisions.	*HIS _____ 15. HERS _____ 15.
My family has had financial problems as long as I can remember.	*HIS _____ 16. HERS _____ 16.

My parents were very careful in their use of credit cards.	*HIS _____ 17. HERS _____ 17.
We considered working more important than time with the family.	*HIS _____ 18. HERS _____ 18.
In my family, we used coupons.	*HIS _____ 19. HERS _____ 19.
My mother handled the household bills.	*HIS _____ 20. HERS _____ 20.
Gambling was not an acceptable use of money.	*HIS _____ 21. HERS _____ 21.
My father paid the bill when we went out to a restaurant or hotel.	*HIS _____ 22. HERS _____ 22.
Having the latest styles of clothing was very important to my family.	*HIS _____ 23. HERS _____ 23.
My family believed it was important to pay all the bills when they were due.	*HIS _____ 24. HERS _____ 24.
My mother would give us money and say, "Now, don't tell your father."	*HIS _____ 25. HERS _____ 25.

You have completed the family statements. On pages 123–125 you will answer statements concerning you and your spouse-to-be. Respond to the statements as you have in this set of worksheets, answering first for yourself and then as you think your spouse-to-be would answer.

"HER" WORKSHEET II

I think it is okay to declare bankruptcy.	HIS ____ 1. *HERS ____ 1.
It is important to me that we have a budget and try to live within it.	HIS ____ 2. *HERS ____ 2.
I have clear goals of what possessions I'd like to buy.	HIS ____ 3. *HERS ____ 3.
I think we should make our children save money.	HIS ____ 4. *HERS ____ 4.
I believe we should recycle things like newspapers and aluminum cans.	HIS ____ 5. *HERS ____ 5.
I think we should shop for lower prices whenever possible.	HIS ____ 6. *HERS ____ 6.
I think it is important that the wife establish credit in her own name.	HIS ____ 7. *HERS ____ 7.
Credit card balances should be paid off each month.	HIS ____ 8. *HERS ____ 8.
All our money should go into the same pot and all expenses be shared.	HIS ____ 9. *HERS ____ 9.
I think it is important that we each have our own savings account.	HIS ____ 10. *HERS ____ 10.
I think it is okay to ask our parents for financial help.	HIS ____ 11. *HERS ____ 11.
Children need to have money of their own to spend.	HIS ____ 12. *HERS ____ 12.
I think it is important that we have a will drawn up after we get married.	HIS ____ 13. *HERS ____ 13.
Credit cards should be used only in emergencies.	HIS ____ 14. *HERS ____ 14.
Vacations are more important to me than saving money.	HIS ____ 15. *HERS ____ 15.
I will go into debt to buy a house.	HIS ____ 16. *HERS ____ 16.

I do not believe it is necessary to let our children know our financial condition.	HIS ____ 17. *HERS ____ 17.
I think we should together plan the cost of our wedding and honeymoon.	HIS ____ 18. *HERS ____ 18.
I think I am the one who should control the money in our marriage.	HIS ____ 19. *HERS ____ 19.
I always balance my checkbook to the penny.	HIS ____ 20. *HERS ____ 20.
I think it is important to save for the future.	HIS ____ 21. *HERS ____ 21.
I think gambling is okay.	HIS ____ 22. *HERS ____ 22.
It is important for me to have some money for which I don't have to be responsible to you.	HIS ____ 23. *HERS ____ 23.
I like to carry a lot of money with me most of the time.	HIS ____ 24. *HERS ____ 24.
We should have two checking accounts—yours and mine.	HIS ____ 25. *HERS ____ 25.
I would not borrow money from my friends.	HIS ____ 26. *HERS ____ 26.
The female should have to pay for all the wedding bills.	HIS ____ 27. *HERS ____ 27.
Men should always make more money than women.	HIS ____ 28. *HERS ____ 28.
It will bother me a lot if I have to ask you for money all the time.	HIS ____ 29. *HERS ____ 29.
I think I should be able to lend money to a friend or relative without asking you.	HIS ____ 30. *HERS ____ 30.
I am unconcerned about money and tend not to worry about financial matters.	HIS ____ 31. *HERS ____ 31.
I would not like it if my mate made more money than I made.	HIS ____ 32. *HERS ____ 32.
I want to talk with you about how we spend our money.	HIS ____ 33. *HERS ____ 33.

Time together with you is more important to me than a high-paying job with long hours, as long as we have enough money to meet our needs.	HIS _____ 34. *HERS _____ 34.
It would upset me to find out my marriage partner had money or debts I didn't know about.	HIS _____ 35. *HERS _____ 35.
I believe it is important for us to tithe.	HIS _____ 36. *HERS _____ 36.
I know very little about money matters and would like my marriage partner to handle it.	HIS _____ 37. *HERS _____ 37.
I believe the male has the primary role to provide for the needs of the family.	HIS _____ 38. *HERS _____ 38.
I want to eat at a restaurant at least once a week.	HIS _____ 39. *HERS _____ 39.
I will tip only 15 percent at a restaurant, and then only if it was good service.	HIS _____ 40. *HERS _____ 40.
I want us and our children to have the latest fashions if we can afford them.	HIS _____ 41. *HERS _____ 41.
I am willing to listen to my spouse-to-be about money, now and after marriage.	HIS _____ 42. *HERS _____ 42.
It is very important to me that we be honest regarding how we spend our money.	HIS _____ 43. *HERS _____ 43.
I think we should help our parents in their old age if at all possible.	HIS _____ 44. *HERS _____ 44.
I would be willing to move our household because of a job transfer.	HIS _____ 45. *HERS _____ 45.
I think leftovers should be eaten and not thrown away.	HIS _____ 46. *HERS _____ 46.
The thought that we may need to borrow money doesn't bother me.	HIS _____ 47. *HERS _____ 47.
I believe it is important to pay the bills on time.	HIS _____ 48. *HERS _____ 48.
I think the husband should handle all family investments.	HIS _____ 49. *HERS _____ 49.
I believe it is important to keep God's instructions about money foremost in our decisions.	HIS _____ 50. *HERS _____ 50.

You have completed the couple statements.

"HIS" WORKSHEET II

I think it is okay to declare bankruptcy.	*HIS ____ 1. HERS ____ 1.
It is important to me that we have a budget and try to live within it.	*HIS ____ 2. HERS ____ 2.
I have clear goals of what possessions I'd like to buy.	*HIS ____ 3. HERS ____ 3.
I think we should make our children save money.	*HIS ____ 4. HERS ____ 4.
I believe we should recycle things like newspapers and aluminum cans.	*HIS ____ 5. HERS ____ 5.
I think we should shop for lower prices whenever possible.	*HIS ____ 6. HERS ____ 6.
I think it is important that the wife establish credit in her own name.	*HIS ____ 7. HERS ____ 7.
Credit card balances should be paid off each month.	*HIS ____ 8. HERS ____ 8.
All our money should go into the same pot and all expenses be shared.	*HIS ____ 9. HERS ____ 9.
I think it is important that we each have our own savings account.	*HIS ____ 10. HERS ____ 10.
I think it is okay to ask our parents for financial help.	*HIS ____ 11. HERS ____ 11.
Children need to have money of their own to spend.	*HIS ____ 12. HERS ____ 12.
I think it is important that we have a will drawn up after we get married.	*HIS ____ 13. HERS ____ 13.
Credit cards should be used only in emergencies.	*HIS ____ 14. HERS ____ 14.
Vacations are more important to me than saving money.	*HIS ____ 15. HERS ____ 15.
I will go into debt to buy a house.	*HIS ____ 16. HERS ____ 16.

I do not believe it is necessary to let our children know our financial condition.	*HIS ____ 17. HERS ____ 17.
I think we should together plan the cost of our wedding and honeymoon.	*HIS ____ 18. HERS ____ 18.
I think I am the one who should control the money in our marriage.	*HIS ____ 19. HERS ____ 19.
I always balance my checkbook to the penny.	*HIS ____ 20. HERS ____ 20.
I think it is important to save for the future.	*HIS ____ 21. HERS ____ 21.
I think gambling is okay.	*HIS ____ 22. HERS ____ 22.
It is important for me to have some money for which I don't have to be responsible to you.	*HIS ____ 23. HERS ____ 23.
I like to carry a lot of money with me most of the time.	*HIS ____ 24. HERS ____ 24.
We should have two checking accounts—yours and mine.	*HIS ____ 25. HERS ____ 25.
I would not borrow money from my friends.	*HIS ____ 26. HERS ____ 26.
The female should have to pay for all the wedding bills.	*HIS ____ 27. HERS ____ 27.
Men should always make more money than women.	*HIS ____ 28. HERS ____ 28.
It will bother me a lot if I have to ask you for money all the time.	*HIS ____ 29. HERS ____ 29.
I think I should be able to lend money to a friend or relative without asking you.	*HIS ____ 30. HERS ____ 30.
I am unconcerned about money and tend not to worry about financial matters.	*HIS ____ 31. HERS ____ 31.
I would not like it if my mate made more money than I made.	*HIS ____ 32. HERS ____ 32.
I want to talk with you about how we spend our money.	*HIS ____ 33. HERS ____ 33.

Time together with you is more important to me than a high-paying job with long hours, as long as we have enough money to meet our needs.	*HIS _____ 34. HERS _____ 34.
It would upset me to find out my marriage partner had money or debts I didn't know about.	*HIS _____ 35. HERS _____ 35.
I believe it is important for us to tithe.	*HIS _____ 36. HERS _____ 36.
I know very little about money matters and would like my marriage partner to handle it.	*HIS _____ 37. HERS _____ 37.
I believe the male has the primary role to provide for the needs of the family.	*HIS _____ 38. HERS _____ 38.
I want to eat at a restaurant at least once a week.	*HIS _____ 39. HERS _____ 39.
I will tip only 15 percent at a restaurant, and then only if it was good service.	*HIS _____ 40. HERS _____ 40.
I want us and our children to have the latest fashions if we can afford them.	*HIS _____ 41. HERS _____ 41.
I am willing to listen to my spouse-to-be about money, now and after marriage.	*HIS _____ 42. HERS _____ 42.
It is very important to me that we be honest regarding how we spend our money.	*HIS _____ 43. HERS _____ 43.
I think we should help our parents in their old age if at all possible.	*HIS _____ 44. HERS _____ 44.
I would be willing to move our household because of a job transfer.	*HIS _____ 45. HERS _____ 45.
I think leftovers should be eaten and not thrown away.	*HIS _____ 46. HERS _____ 46.
The thought that we may need to borrow money doesn't bother me.	*HIS _____ 47. HERS _____ 47.
I believe it is important to pay the bills on time.	*HIS _____ 48. HERS _____ 48.
I think the husband should handle all family investments.	*HIS _____ 49. HERS _____ 49.
I believe it is important to keep God's instructions about money foremost in our decisions.	*HIS _____ 50. HERS _____ 50.

You have completed the couple statements.

MONEY MATTERS COMMUNICATION
AND PERCEPTION EVALUATION

1. To evaluate the family money matters section, compare your answers in both the "His" and "Hers" spaces from Worksheet I and give yourselves one point for each answer that is the same. There is a total of 50 points, two points for each statement. This is your communication and perception score for your families.

   Family Communication and Perception Score _____

2. To evaluate the couple money matters section, compare your answers in both the "His" and "Hers" spaces from Worksheet II and give yourselves one point for each answer that is the same. There is a total of 100 points, two points for each statement. This is your communication and perception score as a couple.

   Couple Communication and Perception Score _____

   Total Family and Couple Communication and Perception Score _____

   125–150 A score between 125 and 150 indicates that you have good communication and in many areas your perceptions are the same.

   100–124 A score between 100 and 124 indicates that you may not have spent enough time together sharing your thoughts and feelings about yourselves and your families. Be open and honest with one another in these areas and set aside more time for serious talks.

   0–99 If your score falls below 100, you have much to learn about each other and your families. Communication is the key to a good relationship. You must begin sharing your thoughts and feelings in order to know how you agree and disagree.

In this evaluation, you have established the level of communication and perception you have in your relationship about money matters.

PROBLEM AREAS EVALUATION

To evaluate your problem areas or those areas requiring more attention, compare your answers in the following manner:

1. Take only the answers from the "*His" space on "His" Worksheet II and compare them to the answers from the "*Hers" space on "Her" Worksheet II. These are your answers about yourselves.

2. Compare these answers and give yourselves one point for each answer that is the same. There is a total of 50 points. This is your couple problem area score.

Couple Problem Area Score_____

40–50   A score between 40 and 50 indicates that you have some areas to discuss further but you are similar in most ways. Remember to seek a solution to your differences.

0–39   A score of less than 40 indicates that your backgrounds, your values, and your beliefs may not be compatible. You need to take more time to talk and, perhaps, to see a counselor before going on with marriage plans. Problem areas that are present before marriage will not just magically disappear after marriage.

Do not consider Worksheet I in the evaluation of problem areas for you as a couple.

PRIORITIES AND MONEY

Below are listed some items that may be a financial priority for you and your spouse-to-be. Each line to the right of the items represents how much importance you and your future spouse now give to the item when it comes to making decisions about spending your money after marriage. Men place an *X* on the line to show how important the item is for you, and women place an *0* on the line to indicate how important the item is.

	Low Priority					High Priority				
Automobiles	1	2	3	4	5	6	7	8	9	10
Buying a house	1	2	3	4	5	6	7	8	9	10
Charities	1	2	3	4	5	6	7	8	9	10
Church	1	2	3	4	5	6	7	8	9	10
Clothes	1	2	3	4	5	6	7	8	9	10
Club membership	1	2	3	4	5	6	7	8	9	10
Education	1	2	3	4	5	6	7	8	9	10
Food	1	2	3	4	5	6	7	8	9	10
Furniture	1	2	3	4	5	6	7	8	9	10
Gifts for our families	1	2	3	4	5	6	7	8	9	10
Having children	1	2	3	4	5	6	7	8	9	10
Health care	1	2	3	4	5	6	7	8	9	10
Helping family	1	2	3	4	5	6	7	8	9	10
Hobbies	1	2	3	4	5	6	7	8	9	10
Insurance	1	2	3	4	5	6	7	8	9	10
Investments	1	2	3	4	5	6	7	8	9	10
New furniture	1	2	3	4	5	6	7	8	9	10
Recreational activities	1	2	3	4	5	6	7	8	9	10
Reducing debts	1	2	3	4	5	6	7	8	9	10
Retirement	1	2	3	4	5	6	7	8	9	10
Savings	1	2	3	4	5	6	7	8	9	10
Travel	1	2	3	4	5	6	7	8	9	10
Other:	1	2	3	4	5	6	7	8	9	10

Now discuss your answers. Are any of your *Xs* and *Os* far apart? Spend enough time talking through these issues to understand why certain items are so important to you and your spouse-to-be.

ANSWER THE FOLLOWING MONEY QUESTIONS TOGETHER

1. Will you both work after marriage? After the children are born?
2. Who managed the money at home (mother/father)?
3. Who will manage your money?
4. Do you plan to save money each month? How much?
5. How soon do you plan to buy a house? How much money will you need to put down?
6. Do you have insurance: life, medical, household, car? How much do you need?
7. Are you a spender or a saver? What about your spouse-to-be?
8. How many credit cards are too many?
9. What is "fun money"?
10. Will the wife and husband have separate checking and savings accounts?
11. How will God's teachings be a part of your money decisions?

FIRST YEAR FINANCIAL GOALS

In the space below, describe what you see as the financial goals for the first year of your marriage. Decide together what your goals will be.

HERS: FINANCIAL CONDITION

Now is not the time for financial secrets. Before you marry, it is important that each of you know the financial condition of the other. Fill out this form as completely as you can. Then discuss it as you plan your budget together. Be as open and honest as you can.

Assets

AMOUNTS IN:

Savings	$_____
Checking	$_____
Real estate owned	$_____
US Savings Bonds	$_____
Life insurance (cash value)	$_____
Other investments	$_____
TOTAL	$_____

INCOME:

Salary (monthly)	$_____
Dividends	$_____
Bonus	$_____
Rental property income	$_____
Other	$_____
TOTAL	$_____

Liabilities

	Monthly Payments	Total Amount Due	Pay Off Date
AUTOMOBILE	$_____	$_____	_____
MORTGAGE/RENT	$_____	$_____	_____
CREDIT CARDS:	$_____	$_____	_____
Master Card	$_____	$_____	_____
Visa	$_____	$_____	_____

American Express $_____ $_____   _____

Other $_____ $_____   _____

DENTAL BILLS $_____ $_____   _____

MEDICAL BILLS $_____ $_____   _____

INSURANCE:

  Car $_____ $_____   _____

  Dental $_____ $_____   _____

  Life $_____ $_____   _____

  Health $_____ $_____   _____

  Home $_____ $_____   _____

PERSONAL DEBTS:

  Friends $_____ $_____   _____

  Relatives $_____ $_____   _____

  Coworkers $_____ $_____   _____

  Bank $_____ $_____   _____

TAXES DUE:

  Income $_____ $_____   _____

  Property tax $_____ $_____   _____

OTHER LOANS $_____ $_____   _____

TOTAL $_____ $_____   _____

HIS: FINANCIAL CONDITION

Now is not the time for financial secrets. Before you marry, it is important that each of you know the financial condition of the other. Fill out this form as completely as you can. Then discuss it as you plan your budget together. Be as open and honest as you can.

Assets

AMOUNTS IN:

Savings	$_____
Checking	$_____
Real estate owned	$_____
US Savings Bonds	$_____
Life insurance (cash value)	$_____
Other investments	$_____
TOTAL	$_____

INCOME:

Salary (monthly)	$_____
Dividends	$_____
Bonus	$_____
Rental property income	$_____
Other	$_____
TOTAL	$_____

Liabilities

	Monthly Payments	Total Amount Due	Pay Off Date
AUTOMOBILE	$_____	$_____	_____
MORTGAGE/RENT	$_____	$_____	_____
CREDIT CARDS:	$_____	$_____	_____
Master Card	$_____	$_____	_____
Visa	$_____	$_____	_____

American Express	$_____	$_____	_____
Other	$_____	$_____	_____
DENTAL BILLS	$_____	$_____	_____
MEDICAL BILLS	$_____	$_____	_____
INSURANCE:			
Car	$_____	$_____	_____
Dental	$_____	$_____	_____
Life	$_____	$_____	_____
Health	$_____	$_____	_____
Home	$_____	$_____	_____
PERSONAL DEBTS:			
Friends	$_____	$_____	_____
Relatives	$_____	$_____	_____
Coworkers	$_____	$_____	_____
Bank	$_____	$_____	_____
TAXES DUE:			
Income	$_____	$_____	_____
Property tax	$_____	$_____	_____
OTHER LOANS	$_____	$_____	_____
TOTAL	$_____	$_____	_____

FINANCIAL COVENANT

Place your initials in the space following the responsibilities you agree to assume in the Financial Covenant.

Marriage is a covenant to be open, honest, faithful, and permanent. You both must be clear about your expectations, priorities, responsibilities, and ways of handling your finances before you enter marriage.

1.	I agree that money will never be more important than our relationship.		
2.	I agree to let you know if I think either of us is becoming irresponsible about financial matters.		
3.	I agree to always be open and honest about financial matters.		
4.	I agree to stay within the budget we plan together.		
5.	I agree that from the day of our wedding, money is ours and the problems and joys it brings are also ours to share.		
6.	I agree to work with you until we agree how to pay and who will pay the bills.		
7.	I agree to make my wants and my needs a matter of our wants and our needs from this day forward.		
8.	I agree to consult with you before making a major purchase.		
9.	I agree that credit cards can be a major problem, and I'll always talk to you before making a purchase over $ _____.		
10.	I have shared with you to the best of my knowledge all my assets and outstanding debts to this date.		
11.	I agree to look at money as a tool to be used for the betterment of both of us.		
12.	I agree to take responsibility for how I handle our finances.		

13. We have identified some statements about money that we should take more time to discuss. I agree to set aside time to discuss with you the following: • _____ • _____ • _____ • _____ • _____		
14. I agree that if, for any reason, our financial situation ever becomes a problem that we cannot handle, I will go with you to get professional help.		
15. I believe that God's teaching and guidelines concerning money are important, and I agree to make them a part of our marriage.		

I agree to this Financial Covenant because I love and respect you and want only the best for us in our marriage relationship.

Her signature: _____

I agree to this Financial Covenant because I love and respect you and want only the best for us in our marriage relationship.

His signature: _____

SEXUAL RELATIONSHIP

· · · · · · · · ·

Touching, holding, and hugging are not something you should do; they're something you must do to communicate your love for one another.

Although we know that good communication is required for a good marriage, the one area in which we communicate with each other the least seems to be in our sexual relationship. No one, male or female, is a mind reader. To meet the needs of your mate, each of you must be free and willing to express yourself openly and honestly in all areas of your relationship.

Over the years our society has made sex something not to be talked about — not in the family, not in the schools, and certainly not in the church. If sex was discussed, it was usually in an embarrassing, humorous, or coarse context; or it was described as a duty, something you just had to put up with. The problem is that our society has narrowed its thinking of sexual relationships to just one thing: *intercourse.*

Your sexual relationship is much more than *just* intercourse. Intercourse without the freedom to share, to enjoy, to love, is no longer a sexual relationship. It then becomes a duty.

UNDERSTANDING YOUR SEXUALITY

It is important to understand that God holds a very high view of our sexuality. The Bible teaches this. The first chapter of Genesis tells us God created us "male and female," in His image, for one another and having the capacity to love and be loved in a special way. God gives His blessings on our sexual relationships within the confines of a covenant relationship (marriage). In a covenant relationship, our sexual relationship can be as God intended: for male and female to "become one flesh."

If you begin now communicating openly and honestly about your sexual relationship, you will be more likely to continue this practice throughout your marriage. It is helpful not only to understand and discuss God's perspective on sexuality but also to learn as much as possible about your body and the body of your future spouse and to discuss that as well.

Before marrying, you both need to schedule a visit with a physician. Your appointment should involve a physical for both of you, and include a pelvic examination for the woman. Take time to discuss any questions or concerns you may have regarding your sexual relationship, such as how are you really put together and how do you function.

A good sexual relationship begins with accurate, intelligent information about your body and the body of your mate. Sex is the one area our society has talked and communicated least about in a healthy way. Ask your doctor about sexual intercourse and the sexual response cycle, the menstruation cycle, birth control, and childbirth. You are not born knowing how to be a good lover, a good husband or a good wife in the area of sexual relations. The more you know, the less sexual fumbling you will do.

After you marry, sexual communication between you and your spouse will be critical. Sexual needs, responses, and enjoyments change through the years. We all have differences — likes and dislikes. You need to be able to communicate these to your spouse if you are to grow, change, and please each other. Begin now talking freely and being as creative, adventurous, love-giving, and love-receiving as possible.

Touching is one of the most important ways of communicating. Touching, holding, and hugging are not something you *should* do; they are something you *must* do to communicate your love for one another. Doctors tell us that if a baby is not touched and held, the baby will not feel secure. To be healthy and happy, we must touch and be touched.

The more you touch and hold someone, the more you feel your love for them. The more you love someone, the more you touch and hold them. Love grows and flourishes like a plant. The more you see that the plant receives water, food, care, and sunshine, the better it grows and the healthier it becomes. The love in a relationship also has needs—needs for touching, holding, kissing, caring, and sharing—that must be filled for the love to grow and flourish. Without these needs being met, the love—and the plant—will wither and die. Your sexual relationship isn't just what happens when you make love, but what happens all day long as you interact together. The loving glances, the smile, the sharing of feelings—all of these help to nurture your sexual relationship.

So communicate your needs, what makes you happy and what pleases you. Talk about positions, frequency, where to touch, and where not to. Give each other the freedom to express yourselves. Enjoy your differences. Accept the differences in your needs. Your mate's needs are not statements about your adequacy. As you accept those needs, you will communicate your acceptance of your mate.

You should always remember that force, or seeking only to meet your needs, does not create or stimulate the growth of love. Instead, it threatens and may destroy it. It is also important to realize that if you are interested in a good sexual relationship, you must not use sex as a weapon or reward.

Men and women are different. God made us this way. What makes you happy may not fulfill your partner's needs for happiness. Each of us is responsible for our own needs being met, and we can do this by communicating those needs to our spouse.

Sexual relationships flourish and grow with special words, glances, and touches. Women need to be held more and shown they are loved without always having intercourse. You need always to communicate—in bed and out of bed—that you love one another and you are special to each other. You are individuals, but one together in your relationship. Your happiness *as a couple* is #1. Your happiness as *individuals* is #2.

Because lovemaking is not always talked about or taught at home, school, or church, we are left to learn through trial and error. Men and women become better lovers and have more sensual experiences when they find, through experience, what arouses and pleases one another. Our likes, dislikes, and senses are unique to each of us. But there are basic requirements for all of us to experience pleasure.

Kissing, touching, caressing, holding, and petting: all of these are stimulants that relax and prepare us for lovemaking. This is what we refer to as foreplay. On your honeymoon and throughout your marriage, you should be sure to give yourselves plenty of time for this and to explore what is pleasing to one another in lovemaking.

God gave both the male and the female sensitive areas to stimulate such as lips, breasts, and genitals, making the sexual relationship pleasing for both, not just for the male. Many men and women are unaware that the clitoris (a small bean-shaped organ at the front and top of a woman's genitals) is the source of sexual stimulation for the woman, just as the penis is for the man. The clitoris must be stimulated and aroused for a woman to experience an orgasm.

The key to sexual satisfaction is taking the time to communicate during love-making. It is a step and signal communication process. The willingness to guide and be guided to pleasure is part of the process. The woman—by gently leading her lover and giving him guidance in what pleases her—can greatly increase her pleasure and excitement as well as that of her husband. The same is true for the man. Because of our differences, we need to be aware of one another's likes and dislikes and willing to please.

Communicate and guide with *do's*, not *don'ts*; with phrases such as, "This pleases me," rather than "I don't like that." Try communicating with "Honey, it really pleases me when you touch me here," or "Honey, it really pleases me when you do this!"

For too long we have been educated either by Hollywood movies, television, and novels or by no one at all. So remember that your sexual relationship and how you please your partner is something you learn together. Sexual intimacy is important for you and your mate. It is not something to be shared openly with the world. Sexual knowledge to benefit others should be shared and taught, but your private, intimate sexual relationship is yours and yours alone. If you and your mate find that you have problems in your intimate sexual relationship, go together to consult a professional marriage therapist.

Keep in mind that all of the ways you respond to your mate are ways you have learned. If your family didn't hug, you probably will not hug. If your family shared their feelings openly, so will you. You both come from families who express them-selves differently. You must now learn to communicate with each other.

SEXUAL RELATING

The following statements on the "Her" Worksheets I and II and the "His" Worksheets I and II, pages 142–151, are about the way you and your families communicate about sexual relationships. In our sexual relationship, do we hug, touch, kiss, talk, and communicate about our likes and dislikes, or do we not? The more you know about each other and your families of origin, the more you will understand how to please one another. Meeting your mate's needs, and knowing your own, comes from understanding and communication.

Sexual information in families is most often communicated by nonverbal messages. When responding to the following statements, think about not only what was said but also what wasn't said. Again, you will respond *T* and *F* to these statements as you have in previous sessions.

"HER" WORKSHEET I

My father believed that sex was a cure for every problem with my mother.	HIS ____ 1. *HERS ____ 1.
My mother and father had a loving relationship.	HIS ____ 2. *HERS ____ 2.
In my family, sex was not discussed.	HIS ____ 3. *HERS ____ 3.
Dirty jokes and foul language were all right for the men in our family to use.	HIS ____ 4. *HERS ____ 4.
My parents slept in separate beds.	HIS ____ 5. *HERS ____ 5.
My mother and father hugged and kissed in front of the children.	HIS ____ 6. *HERS ____ 6.
My parents frequently complimented one another on their appearance.	HIS ____ 7. *HERS ____ 7.
I always knew that my parents loved me.	HIS ____ 8. *HERS ____ 8.
In my family, it was okay for women to cry, but not okay for men.	HIS ____ 9. *HERS ____ 9.
My family had a different sexual standard for men than for women.	HIS ____ 10. *HERS ____ 10.
My mother thought intercourse was a wife's duty.	HIS ____ 11. *HERS ____ 11.
My parents believed that a marriage should be faithful and permanent.	HIS ____ 12. *HERS ____ 12.
The women in my family do not use foul language.	HIS ____ 13. *HERS ____ 13.
My family was very physically affectionate, with kissing, hugging, and touching.	HIS ____ 14. *HERS ____ 14.
In my family, we only discussed sexual issues with my mother.	HIS ____ 15. *HERS ____ 15.
In my family, there were two sets of sex rules—one for boys and one for girls.	HIS ____ 16. *HERS ____ 16.

My family used affection as a reward for good behavior and withheld it as punishment for bad behavior.	HIS _____ 17. *HERS _____ 17.
My father frequently told my mother that she was his sweetheart.	HIS _____ 18. *HERS _____ 18.
I received excellent sexual information from my parents.	HIS _____ 19. *HERS _____ 19.
My mother and father fought about sex frequently.	HIS _____ 20. *HERS _____ 20.
I never felt free to ask my parents anything about sexual issues.	HIS _____ 21. *HERS _____ 21.
My parents always put each other first.	HIS _____ 22. *HERS _____ 22.
My family displayed affection toward me.	HIS _____ 23. *HERS _____ 23.
There was a lot of laughter and fun in my family.	HIS _____ 24. *HERS _____ 24.
My parents responded to my developing sexuality in a positive way.	HIS _____ 25. *HERS _____ 25.

You have completed the family statements. On pages 146–148 you will answer statements concerning you and your spouse-to-be. Respond to the statements as you have in this set of worksheets, answering first for yourself and then as you think your spouse-to-be would answer.

"HIS" WORKSHEET I

My father believed that sex was a cure for every problem with my mother.	*HIS ____ 1.	HERS ____ 1.
My mother and father had a loving relationship.	*HIS ____ 2.	HERS ____ 2.
In my family, sex was not discussed.	*HIS ____ 3.	HERS ____ 3.
Dirty jokes and foul language were all right for the men in our family to use.	*HIS ____ 4.	HERS ____ 4.
My parents slept in separate beds.	*HIS ____ 5.	HERS ____ 5.
My mother and father hugged and kissed in front of the children.	*HIS ____ 6.	HERS ____ 6.
My parents frequently complimented one another on their appearance.	*HIS ____ 7.	HERS ____ 7.
I always knew that my parents loved me.	*HIS ____ 8.	HERS ____ 8.
In my family, it was okay for women to cry, but not okay for men.	*HIS ____ 9.	HERS ____ 9.
My family had a different sexual standard for men than for women.	*HIS ____ 10.	HERS ____ 10.
My mother thought intercourse was a wife's duty.	*HIS ____ 11.	HERS ____ 11.
My parents believed that a marriage should be faithful and permanent.	*HIS ____ 12.	HERS ____ 12.
The women in my family do not use foul language.	*HIS ____ 13.	HERS ____ 13.
My family was very physically affectionate, with kissing, hugging, and touching.	*HIS ____ 14.	HERS ____ 14.
In my family, we only discussed sexual issues with my mother.	*HIS ____ 15.	HERS ____ 15.
In my family, there were two sets of sex rules—one for boys and one for girls.	*HIS ____ 16.	HERS ____ 16.

My family used affection as a reward for good behavior and withheld it as punishment for bad behavior.	*HIS _____ 17. HERS _____ 17.
My father frequently told my mother that she was his sweetheart.	*HIS _____ 18. HERS _____ 18.
I received excellent sexual information from my parents.	*HIS _____ 19. HERS _____ 19.
My mother and father fought about sex frequently.	*HIS _____ 20. HERS _____ 20.
I never felt free to ask my parents anything about sexual issues.	*HIS _____ 21. HERS _____ 21.
My parents always put each other first.	*HIS _____ 22. HERS _____ 22.
My family displayed affection toward me.	*HIS _____ 23. HERS _____ 23.
There was a lot of laughter and fun in my family.	*HIS _____ 24. HERS _____ 24.
My parents responded to my developing sexuality in a positive way.	*HIS _____ 25. HERS _____ 25.

You have completed the family statements. On pages 149–151 you will answer statements concerning you and your spouse-to-be. Respond to the statements as you have in this set of worksheets, answering first for yourself and then as you think your spouse-to-be would answer.

"HER" WORKSHEET II

In our marriage the wife should always be willing to submit to the husband's sexual needs.	HIS ____ 1. *HERS ____ 1.
I understand that the sexual things I do may not always be pleasing to my mate and want him to share with me his discomfort with that activity.	HIS ____ 2. *HERS ____ 2.
I want to please my spouse-to-be, so I talk openly and honestly with him.	HIS ____ 3. *HERS ____ 3.
I think it is important that we continue to "date" each other after we are married.	HIS ____ 4. *HERS ____ 4.
I believe it is important to be physically clean for my mate.	HIS ____ 5. *HERS ____ 5.
I understand that men and women have different needs.	HIS ____ 6. *HERS ____ 6.
I believe sex is only for having children.	HIS ____ 7. *HERS ____ 7.
I think there are some nonacceptable forms of sexual activities.	HIS ____ 8. *HERS ____ 8.
I believe God intended sex to be only within the marriage relationship.	HIS ____ 9. *HERS ____ 9.
I believe that learning more about my mate's needs will enrich our sexual relationship after marriage.	HIS ____ 10. *HERS ____ 10.
I believe that faithfulness in a marriage is absolutely necessary.	HIS ____ 11. *HERS ____ 11.
I believe my partner and I should communicate so that we really know what is pleasing to each other.	HIS ____ 12. *HERS ____ 12.
I am comfortable with my body.	HIS ____ 13. *HERS ____ 13.
I think it is important to "set the mood" for lovemaking with music, candles, flowers.	HIS ____ 14. *HERS ____ 14.
I was sexually abused as a child.	HIS ____ 15. *HERS ____ 15.
It is important to me that we greet each other affectionately after being apart all day.	HIS ____ 16. *HERS ____ 16.

I have some fear of sex.	HIS _____ 17. *HERS _____ 17.
I believe that it is all right for the woman to guide the man to what pleases her.	HIS _____ 18. *HERS _____ 18.
I think that sex outside of marriage is okay with my spouse-to-be.	HIS _____ 19. *HERS _____ 19.
I believe that if my mate doesn't like what I do sexually, he should let me do it anyway.	HIS _____ 20. *HERS _____ 20.
I believe that men think more often about sex than women.	HIS _____ 21. *HERS _____ 21.
I feel free to talk about my mate and our intimate sex life with my friends.	HIS _____ 22. *HERS _____ 22.
I think I would be able to forgive my mate's continuous unfaithfulness.	HIS _____ 23. *HERS _____ 23.
I believe that dirty movies or books are not good for a healthy marriage.	HIS _____ 24. *HERS _____ 24.
I am comfortable with my spouse-to-be showing affection in public.	HIS _____ 25. *HERS _____ 25.
It is easy for me to talk about sex and our sexual relationship with my spouse-to-be.	HIS _____ 26. *HERS _____ 26.
I think it's okay to use sex as a weapon or reward.	HIS _____ 27. *HERS _____ 27.
I believe that birth control is completely the woman's responsibility.	HIS _____ 28. *HERS _____ 28.
I think I need to lose weight.	HIS _____ 29. *HERS _____ 29.
I am uncomfortable with dirty jokes.	HIS _____ 30. *HERS _____ 30.
It is all right for the woman to initiate sexual activity.	HIS _____ 31. *HERS _____ 31.
I believe sex is a special gift that God intended for married people.	HIS _____ 32. *HERS _____ 32.
I like to show my affection for my spouse-to-be in public.	HIS _____ 33. *HERS _____ 33.

I enjoy hugging and kissing passionately.	HIS _____ 34. *HERS _____ 34.
I believe men are less emotional than women.	HIS _____ 35. *HERS _____ 35.
I don't believe women should be made to have sex during their menstrual period.	HIS _____ 36. *HERS _____ 36.
My spouse-to-be compliments me on my appearance.	HIS _____ 37. *HERS _____ 37.
Men know more about the way to please their mate than women.	HIS _____ 38. *HERS _____ 38.
I believe my spouse-to-be and I should both have a physical examination before marriage.	HIS _____ 39. *HERS _____ 39.
I know my future mate loves me.	HIS _____ 40. *HERS _____ 40.
I believe that men should take the lead in sexual intercourse.	HIS _____ 41. *HERS _____ 41.
I will be open and encourage my mate to lead me to what pleases him.	HIS _____ 42. *HERS _____ 42.
I would like to be held and touched without always having intercourse.	HIS _____ 43. *HERS _____ 43.
I think married people should sleep in separate beds.	HIS _____ 44. *HERS _____ 44.
My partner should know what sexually pleases me without my telling him.	HIS _____ 45. *HERS _____ 45.
I am easily embarrassed when I am nude.	HIS _____ 46. *HERS _____ 46.
Sex is too embarrassing for me to talk about.	HIS _____ 47. *HERS _____ 47.
I believe that love is more important than sex.	HIS _____ 48. *HERS _____ 48.
I am confused about how to really please my mate sexually.	HIS _____ 49. *HERS _____ 49.
I believe God intended married couples to have a fulfilling sex life.	HIS _____ 50. *HERS _____ 50.

You have completed the couple statements.

"HIS" WORKSHEET II

In our marriage the wife should always be willing to submit to the husband's sexual needs.	*HIS ____ 1. HERS ____ 1.
I understand that the sexual things I do may not always be pleasing to my mate and want her to share with me her discomfort with that activity.	*HIS ____ 2. HERS ____ 2.
I want to please my spouse-to-be, so I talk openly and honestly with her.	*HIS ____ 3. HERS ____ 3.
I think it is important that we continue to "date" each other after we are married.	*HIS ____ 4. HERS ____ 4.
I believe it is important to be physically clean for my mate.	*HIS ____ 5. HERS ____ 5.
I understand that men and women have different needs.	*HIS ____ 6. HERS ____ 6.
I believe sex is only for having children.	*HIS ____ 7. HERS ____ 7.
I think there are some nonacceptable forms of sexual activities.	*HIS ____ 8. HERS ____ 8.
I believe God intended sex to be only within the marriage relationship.	*HIS ____ 9. HERS ____ 9.
I believe that learning more about my mate's needs will enrich our sexual relationship after marriage.	*HIS ____ 10. HERS ____ 10.
I believe that faithfulness in a marriage is absolutely necessary.	*HIS ____ 11. HERS ____ 11.
I believe my partner and I should communicate so that we really know what is pleasing to each other.	*HIS ____ 12. HERS ____ 12.
I am comfortable with my body.	*HIS ____ 13. HERS ____ 13.
I think it is important to "set the mood" for lovemaking with music, candles, flowers.	*HIS ____ 14. HERS ____ 14.
I was sexually abused as a child.	*HIS ____ 15. HERS ____ 15.
It is important to me that we greet each other affectionately after being apart all day.	*HIS ____ 16. HERS ____ 16.

I have some fear of sex.	*HIS _____ 17. HERS _____ 17.
I believe that it is all right for the woman to guide the man to what pleases her.	*HIS _____ 18. HERS _____ 18.
I think that sex outside of marriage is okay with my spouse-to-be.	*HIS _____ 19. HERS _____ 19.
I believe that if my mate doesn't like what I do sexually, she should let me do it anyway.	*HIS _____ 20. HERS _____ 20.
I believe that men think more often about sex than women.	*HIS _____ 21. HERS _____ 21.
I feel free to talk about my mate and our intimate sex life with my friends.	*HIS _____ 22. HERS _____ 22.
I think I would be able to forgive my mate's continuous unfaithfulness.	*HIS _____ 23. HERS _____ 23.
I believe that dirty movies or books are not good for a healthy marriage.	*HIS _____ 24. HERS _____ 24.
I am comfortable with my spouse-to-be showing affection in public.	*HIS _____ 25. HERS _____ 25.
It is easy for me to talk about sex and our sexual relationship with my spouse-to-be.	*HIS _____ 26. HERS _____ 26.
I think it's okay to use sex as a weapon or reward.	*HIS _____ 27. HERS _____ 27.
I believe that birth control is completely the woman's responsibility.	*HIS _____ 28. HERS _____ 28.
I think I need to lose weight.	*HIS _____ 29. HERS _____ 29.
I am uncomfortable with dirty jokes.	*HIS _____ 30. HERS _____ 30.
It is all right for the woman to initiate sexual activity.	*HIS _____ 31. HERS _____ 31.
I believe sex is a special gift that God intended for married people.	*HIS _____ 32. HERS _____ 32.
I like to show my affection for my spouse-to-be in public.	*HIS _____ 33. HERS _____ 33.

I enjoy hugging and kissing passionately.	*HIS ____ 34. HERS ____ 34.
I believe men are less emotional than women.	*HIS ____ 35. HERS ____ 35.
I don't believe women should be made to have sex during their menstrual period.	*HIS ____ 36. HERS ____ 36.
My spouse-to-be compliments me on my appearance.	*HIS ____ 37. HERS ____ 37.
Men know more about the way to please their mate than women.	*HIS ____ 38. HERS ____ 38.
I believe my spouse-to-be and I should both have a physical examination before marriage.	*HIS ____ 39. HERS ____ 39.
I know my future mate loves me.	*HIS ____ 40. HERS ____ 40.
I believe that men should take the lead in sexual intercourse.	*HIS ____ 41. HERS ____ 41.
I will be open and encourage my mate to lead me to what pleases her.	*HIS ____ 42. HERS ____ 42.
I would like to be held and touched without always having intercourse.	*HIS ____ 43. HERS ____ 43.
I think married people should sleep in separate beds.	*HIS ____ 44. HERS ____ 44.
My partner should know what sexually pleases me without my telling her.	*HIS ____ 45. HERS ____ 45.
I am easily embarrassed when I am nude.	*HIS ____ 46. HERS ____ 46.
Sex is too embarrassing for me to talk about.	*HIS ____ 47. HERS ____ 47.
I believe that love is more important than sex.	*HIS ____ 48. HERS ____ 48.
I am confused about how to really please my mate sexually.	*HIS ____ 49. HERS ____ 49.
I believe God intended married couples to have a fulfilling sex life.	*HIS ____ 50. HERS ____ 50.

You have completed the couple statements.

SEXUAL RELATIONSHIPS COMMUNICATION AND PERCEPTION EVALUATION

1. To evaluate the family sexual relationships section, compare your answers in both the "His" and "Hers" spaces from Worksheet I and give yourselves one point for each answer that is the same. There is a total of 50 points, two points for each statement. This is your communication and perception score for your families.

Family Communication and Perception Score _____

2. To evaluate the couple sexual relationships section, compare your answers in both the "His" and "Hers" spaces from Worksheet II and give yourselves one point for each answer that is the same. There is a total of 100 points, two points for each statement. This is your communication and perception score as a couple.

Couple Communication and Perception Score _____

Total Family and Couple Communication and Perception Score _____

125–150   A score between 125 and 150 indicates that you have good communication and in many areas your perceptions are the same.

100–124   A score between 100 and 124 indicates that you may not have spent enough time together sharing your thoughts and feelings about yourselves and your families. Be open and honest with one another in these areas and set aside more time for serious talks.

0–99   If your score falls below 100, you still have much to learn about each other and your families. Communication is the key to a good relationship. You must begin sharing your thoughts and feelings in order to know how you agree and disagree.

In this evaluation, you have established the level of communication and perception you have in your relationship about sexual matters.

PROBLEM AREAS EVALUATION

To evaluate your problem areas or those areas requiring more attention, compare your answers in the following manner:

1. Take only the answers from the "*His" space on "His" Worksheet II and compare them to the answers from the "*Hers" space on "Her" Worksheet II. These are your answers about yourselves.

2. Compare these answers and give yourselves one point for each answer that is the same. There is a total of 50 points. This is your couple problem area score.

Couple Problem Area Score _____

40–50   A score between 40 and 50 indicates that you have some areas to discuss further but you are similar in most ways. Remember to seek a solution to your differences.

0–39   A score of less than 40 indicates that your backgrounds, your values, and your beliefs may not be compatible. You need to take more time to talk and, perhaps, to see a counselor before going on with marriage plans. Problem areas that are present before marriage will not just magically disappear after marriage.

Do not consider Worksheet I in the evaluation of problem areas for you as a couple.

EXPRESSING PHYSICAL AND SEXUAL PLEASURE

The following list suggests possible activities through which couples can give and receive physical and sexual pleasure. In the appropriate column answer *yes* if you enjoy or think you would enjoy giving or receiving the activity listed. Answer *no* if you dislike or would be opposed to trying that activity. At the bottom of the page there is room for you to add any other activities that do not appear on the list.

"His"		"Her"
1. _____	Hold each other	_____ 1.
2. _____	Take a shower or bath together	_____ 2.
3. _____	Warm each other in bed	_____ 3.
4. _____	Tickle each other	_____ 4.
5. _____	Hold hands	_____ 5.
6. _____	Hug and kiss	_____ 6.
7. _____	Give massages	_____ 7.
8. _____	Cuddle close in bed	_____ 8.
9. _____	Warm cold feet	_____ 9.
10. _____	Greet affectionately	_____ 10.
11. _____	Touch affectionately	_____ 11.
12. _____	Engage in sexual intercourse	_____ 12.
13. _____	Enjoy petting and sex play	_____ 13.
14. _____	Hug and kiss passionately	_____ 14.
15. _____	Try new sexual behaviors	_____ 15.
16. _____	Engage in oral-genital sex	_____ 16.
17. _____	Admire body	_____ 17.
18. _____	Help reach orgasm	_____ 18.
19. _____	Set mood for sexual activity (music, candles, flowers)	_____ 19.
20. _____	Write something sexually provocative	_____ 20.
21. _____	Caress body with hands	_____ 21.
22. _____	Caress body with mouth	_____ 22.
23. _____	Wear sexually stimulating clothing	_____ 23.
24. _____	Read something pornographic aloud	_____ 24.
25. _____	Know that she/he enjoyed intercourse with me	_____ 25.
26. _____	Initiate sexual activity	_____ 26.

27. _____	Respond pleasantly to your sexual advances	_____	27.
28. _____	Participate with you in a sexual fantasy	_____	28.
29. _____	Present myself to you in the nude	_____	29.
30. _____	Pillow fights	_____	30.

Other pleasurable activities you would like to give to or receive from your spouse-to-be:

- _____
- _____
- _____
- _____
- _____

Any activities you do not agree on need to be discussed. *Remember*, neither of you should be forced to participate in any activity with which you are uncomfortable. Exploring new activities will bring excitement to your relationship.

SEXUAL RELATIONSHIP COVENANT

Place your initials in the space following the responsibilities you agree to assume in the Sexual Relationship Covenant.

Marriage is a special kind of relationship. It is a covenant to be open, honest, faithful, and permanent. In our sexual relationships we both must be clear about our expectations, responsibilities, and willingness to please each other. In this way we can minimize misunderstandings, misjudging, fumbling, and not really pleasing each other.

1.	I agree that we may differ on many things, and I agree to respect your opinion and feelings.		
2.	I agree to be open and honest about our sexual relationship.		
3.	I will always be willing to let you share with me what pleases you.		

4. I agree to tell you, in the best way I can, what does not please me because I love you and want to have the best sexual relationship we can.		
5. I agree that the only way I can really please you is to let you guide me, and I am willing to do so.		
6. I agree to hold you, hug you, and touch you every day.		
7. I understand that our private, intimate sex life is ours alone, and I agree to respect that.		
8. I agree not to use sex as a weapon or a reward.		
9. I agree not to criticize or make fun of your sexuality.		
10. We have identified some statements about our sexual relationship that we should take more time to discuss. I agree to set aside time to discuss with you the following: • _____ • _____ • _____ • _____ • _____		
11. I agree that if, for any reason, we come to a sexual problem we cannot solve, I will go with you to get professional help.		
12. I believe that God's teaching and guidelines about sexual relationships are important and agree to make them a part of our marriage.		

I agree to this Sexual Relationship Covenant because I love and respect you and want only the best for us in our marriage relationship.

Her signature: _____

I agree to this Sexual Relationship Covenant because I love and respect you and want only the best for us in our marriage relationship.

His signature: _____

FAMILY PLANNING AND CHILDREN

· · · · · · · · ·

While children are a blessing and a joy, they can bring pressure and stress to the marriage relationship and are a heavy responsibility.

A very important consideration before you marry is family and children. Having children is the one time humankind joins with God in His creative process. Through children we are able to be a part of the creation of life. From love comes life.

To many couples, marriage means having children and a family, becoming mothers and fathers. Having children is not only an important part of marriage, but for many it is *the* reason for marriage. In some families, having children means you have reached adult status. Although many couples see children as a necessary element to making a marriage complete, other couples plan to develop their careers and to not have children.

It is very interesting to us that this is an area of responsibility many couples seem to defer coming to terms with. In our work with premarital couples, we hear comments and statements like, "Oh, we'll worry about that later," "I want children, but he/she doesn't right now, but I think he/she will change his/her mind," and "First things first." We believe it is critical to decide before you marry if you plan to have children and how they will fit into your lives. You may feel it is premature to discuss these issues. But knowing how you think and feel now can help prevent frustrations later.

Share with one another your feelings and thoughts about having children and answer these important questions: If you or your spouse cannot have children, what will you do? Is adoption okay, or is it out of the question? What if your child is born with a physical or mental problem? Are there physical, medical, or mental problems in either of your families that could be inherited? How many children are you planning to have? How soon will you begin your family? Who will be responsible for the care and feeding of your child? You? Your spouse? Both of you? Will the mother be expected to work after the birth of a child, or do you believe mothers belong at home?

While children are a blessing and a joy, they can bring pressure and stress to the marriage relationship and are a heavy responsibility. They will challenge you in ways you cannot even begin to imagine. When you are raising your children, you will be required to come to terms, as adults, with the things you didn't settle as children.

Many couples believe children will heal a troubled marriage. But couples have also found they experience a decrease in marital satisfaction after children arrive in the family. Thus it is important that you and your spouse-to-be build a strong, healthy relationship before bringing children into your family. Planning your family needs to be a joint discussion. As mentioned earlier, both of you should have a physical examination before you marry. This is a good time to ask questions about your ability to have children and anything that might keep you from having children.

Consider how you feel about birth control. Who is responsible for that? You will find you have many options for controlling pregnancy. It is usually best if you decide together which is safest and acceptable to both of you. Make sure each of you knows what the other feels and thinks about having children and birth control. And decide together how long you will use birth control before starting a family.

Who you marry is one of the most important decisions you will make in your lifetime and deciding whether you will have children is an important part of that decision. Communicating about children *now*, before marriage, spares you many problems, misunderstandings, and heartaches after marriage.

The following statements on the "Her" Worksheets I and II and the "His" Worksheets I and II, pages 159–168, are about the way each of you and your families think and feel about children, family planning, and birth control. Respond *T* and *F* to these statements as you have in previous sessions.

"HER" WORKSHEET I

My parents can't wait to be grandparents.	HIS ____ 1. *HERS ____ 1.
My parents really wanted children.	HIS ____ 2. *HERS ____ 2.
My parents think there is something wrong with a family that doesn't have children.	HIS ____ 3. *HERS ____ 3.
My grandparents had an important role in our family life.	HIS ____ 4. *HERS ____ 4.
My parents did without things so the children could have what they needed.	HIS ____ 5. *HERS ____ 5.
In my family, we were very casual about being undressed around family members.	HIS ____ 6. *HERS ____ 6.
My parents believe you should have as many children as possible.	HIS ____ 7. *HERS ____ 7.
In my family, children were encouraged to voice their opinions concerning family decisions.	HIS ____ 8. *HERS ____ 8.
In my family, children were given an allowance for doing their chores.	HIS ____ 9. *HERS ____ 9.
I believe my parents raised children the way we should.	HIS ____ 10. *HERS ____ 10.
In my family, everyone ate something different at mealtimes.	HIS ____ 11. *HERS ____ 11.
In my family, sons were treated differently than daughters.	HIS ____ 12. *HERS ____ 12.
Both my mom and dad tried to attend my sports, school, and church functions.	HIS ____ 13. *HERS ____ 13.
Mother stayed home and raised the children.	HIS ____ 14. *HERS ____ 14.
In my family, the father was the person who disciplined the children.	HIS ____ 15. *HERS ____ 15.
My father was gone much of the time.	HIS ____ 16. *HERS ____ 16.

In my family, we had fun together.	HIS ____ 17. *HERS ____ 17.
My father used to tell stories to the children.	HIS ____ 18. *HERS ____ 18.
During my childhood, my father didn't pay much attention to me.	HIS ____ 19. *HERS ____ 19.
My family was very close when I was growing up.	HIS ____ 20. *HERS ____ 20.
My parents would not consider abortion as a method of birth control.	HIS ____ 21. *HERS ____ 21.
In my family, it was okay to spank the children.	HIS ____ 22. *HERS ____ 22.
In my family, my parents would hold and hug the children.	HIS ____ 23. *HERS ____ 23.
In my family, it is important to have children to be a complete family.	HIS ____ 24. *HERS ____ 24.
In my family, my parents would get angry and slap the children.	HIS ____ 25. *HERS ____ 25.

You have completed the family statements. On pages 163–165 you will answer statements concerning you and your spouse-to-be. Respond to the statements as you have in this set of worksheets, answering first for yourself and then as you think your spouse-to-be would answer.

"HIS" WORKSHEET I

My parents can't wait to be grandparents.	*HIS ____ 1. HERS ____ 1.
My parents really wanted children.	*HIS ____ 2. HERS ____ 2.
My parents think there is something wrong with a family that doesn't have children.	*HIS ____ 3. HERS ____ 3.
My grandparents had an important role in our family life.	*HIS ____ 4. HERS ____ 4.
My parents did without things so the children could have what they needed.	*HIS ____ 5. HERS ____ 5.
In my family, we were very casual about being undressed around family members.	*HIS ____ 6. HERS ____ 6.
My parents believe you should have as many children as possible.	*HIS ____ 7. HERS ____ 7.
In my family, children were encouraged to voice their opinions concerning family decisions.	*HIS ____ 8. HERS ____ 8.
In my family, children were given an allowance for doing their chores.	*HIS ____ 9. HERS ____ 9.
I believe my parents raised children the way we should.	*HIS ____ 10. HERS ____ 10.
In my family, everyone ate something different at mealtimes.	*HIS ____ 11. HERS ____ 11.
In my family, sons were treated differently than daughters.	*HIS ____ 12. HERS ____ 12.
Both my mom and dad tried to attend my sports, school, and church functions.	*HIS ____ 13. HERS ____ 13.
Mother stayed home and raised the children.	*HIS ____ 14. HERS ____ 14.
In my family, the father was the person who disciplined the children.	*HIS ____ 15. HERS ____ 15.
My father was gone much of the time.	*HIS ____ 16. HERS ____ 16.

In my family, we had fun together.	*HIS ____ 17. HERS ____ 17.
My father used to tell stories to the children.	*HIS ____ 18. HERS ____ 18.
During my childhood, my father didn't pay much attention to me.	*HIS ____ 19. HERS ____ 19.
My family was very close when I was growing up.	*HIS ____ 20. HERS ____ 20.
My parents would not consider abortion as a method of birth control.	*HIS ____ 21. HERS ____ 21.
In my family, it was okay to spank the children.	*HIS ____ 22. HERS ____ 22.
In my family, my parents would hold and hug the children.	*HIS ____ 23. HERS ____ 23.
In my family, it is important to have children to be a complete family.	*HIS ____ 24. HERS ____ 24.
In my family, my parents would get angry and slap the children.	*HIS ____ 25. HERS ____ 25.

You have completed the family statements. On pages 166–168 you will answer statements concerning you and your spouse-to-be. Respond to the statements as you have in this set of worksheets, answering first for yourself and then as you think your spouse-to-be would answer.

"HER" WORKSHEET II

I believe birth control is the responsibility of the female.	HIS ____ 1. *HERS ____ 1.
If we are unable to have children, I would like to adopt.	HIS ____ 2. *HERS ____ 2.
I want to have children after marriage.	HIS ____ 3. *HERS ____ 3.
I think abortion is an acceptable means of birth control.	HIS ____ 4. *HERS ____ 4.
I believe children need to learn how to manage money as they grow up.	HIS ____ 5. *HERS ____ 5.
I think once our children are in school, we should not move.	HIS ____ 6. *HERS ____ 6.
I think it is important for children to be born and raised in the same city.	HIS ____ 7. *HERS ____ 7.
I believe children should make As and Bs in school.	HIS ____ 8. *HERS ____ 8.
I think children should have an allowance.	HIS ____ 9. *HERS ____ 9.
It is important to me to have a daughter.	HIS ____ 10. *HERS ____ 10.
I have some concerns about possible genetic problems in my children.	HIS ____ 11. *HERS ____ 11.
I believe it is all right for children to talk back to their parents.	HIS ____ 12. *HERS ____ 12.
I think it is all right for a woman to smoke and drink when pregnant.	HIS ____ 13. *HERS ____ 13.
I think it is important for children to have pets.	HIS ____ 14. *HERS ____ 14.
I believe the only birth control method to use should be the pill.	HIS ____ 15. *HERS ____ 15.
It is important to me to have a son.	HIS ____ 16. *HERS ____ 16.

It is okay for children to see their parents in the nude.	HIS ____ 17. *HERS ____ 17.
I believe it is okay for the mother to work once children are in elementary school.	HIS ____ 18. *HERS ____ 18.
I believe it is all right to call children names (e.g., dummy, stupid, idiot).	HIS ____ 19. *HERS ____ 19.
It is important to me that we have children as soon as possible.	HIS ____ 20. *HERS ____ 20.
I think it is important that we decide together when to start our family.	HIS ____ 21. *HERS ____ 21.
I believe both father and mother should be involved in the daily care of the children.	HIS ____ 22. *HERS ____ 22.
I think it is important for children to be involved in extra activities (e.g., dancing, sports, art and music lessons).	HIS ____ 23. *HERS ____ 23.
I am not sure I really want to have children.	HIS ____ 24. *HERS ____ 24.
I think reading to children is important.	HIS ____ 25. *HERS ____ 25.
I think it is important for children to know their parents love each other.	HIS ____ 26. *HERS ____ 26.
Children's behavior and manners are very important to me.	HIS ____ 27. *HERS ____ 27.
I think it is important for children to understand Christianity.	HIS ____ 28. *HERS ____ 28.
I believe it is very important for children to know that their parents love them.	HIS ____ 29. *HERS ____ 29.
I believe children should go to church even if they'd rather not.	HIS ____ 30. *HERS ____ 30.
I believe children should have their privacy respected.	HIS ____ 31. *HERS ____ 31.
I believe children should clean their plates.	HIS ____ 32. *HERS ____ 32.
I think it is the responsibility of the parents to teach children about sex and sexuality.	HIS ____ 33. *HERS ____ 33.

I plan to spank our children as a way of discipline.	HIS _____ 34. *HERS _____ 34.	
I believe children should have chores and household jobs to do when they are old enough.	HIS _____ 35. *HERS _____ 35.	
I think sons and daughters should be raised differently.	HIS _____ 36. *HERS _____ 36.	
I believe it is okay for both parents to work.	HIS _____ 37. *HERS _____ 37.	
I believe that larger families are better families.	HIS _____ 38. *HERS _____ 38.	
I want our family to hold and hug each other.	HIS _____ 39. *HERS _____ 39.	
I believe that only female children and women should set the table and wash dishes.	HIS _____ 40. *HERS _____ 40.	
I believe that both the mother and the father should discipline the children.	HIS _____ 41. *HERS _____ 41.	
I believe daily schedules are important for young children.	HIS _____ 42. *HERS _____ 42.	
The number of children we have after marriage is important to me.	HIS _____ 43. *HERS _____ 43.	
I believe children should be told and shown that their parents love them.	HIS _____ 44. *HERS _____ 44.	
It is the parents' responsibility to help children with schoolwork.	HIS _____ 45. *HERS _____ 45.	
The sex of our children is unimportant to me.	HIS _____ 46. *HERS _____ 46.	
I believe it is all right to put off talking about children until after we are married.	HIS _____ 47. *HERS _____ 47.	
I do not plan on having any children at all.	HIS _____ 48. *HERS _____ 48.	
I would like to talk more about the possibility of birth defects in our children and how we would handle that.	HIS _____ 49. *HERS _____ 49.	
I think we could be happy even if we found out we could not have children.	HIS _____ 50. *HERS _____ 50.	

"HIS" WORKSHEET II

I believe birth control is the responsibility of the female.	*HIS _____ 1. HERS _____ 1.
If we are unable to have children, I would like to adopt.	*HIS _____ 2. HERS _____ 2.
I want to have children after marriage.	*HIS _____ 3. HERS _____ 3.
I think abortion is an acceptable means of birth control.	*HIS _____ 4. HERS _____ 4.
I believe children need to learn how to manage money as they grow up.	*HIS _____ 5. HERS _____ 5.
I think once our children are in school, we should not move.	*HIS _____ 6. HERS _____ 6.
I think it is important for children to be born and raised in the same city.	*HIS _____ 7. HERS _____ 7.
I believe children should make As and Bs in school.	*HIS _____ 8. HERS _____ 8.
I think children should have an allowance.	*HIS _____ 9. HERS _____ 9.
It is important to me to have a daughter.	*HIS _____ 10. HERS _____ 10.
I have some concerns about possible genetic problems in my children.	*HIS _____ 11. HERS _____ 11.
I believe it is all right for children to talk back to their parents.	*HIS _____ 12. HERS _____ 12.
I think it is all right for a woman to smoke and drink when pregnant.	*HIS _____ 13. HERS _____ 13.
I think it is important for children to have pets.	*HIS _____ 14. HERS _____ 14.
I believe the only birth control method to use should be the pill.	*HIS _____ 15. HERS _____ 15.
It is important to me to have a son.	*HIS _____ 16. HERS _____ 16.

It is okay for children to see their parents in the nude.	*HIS ____ 17. HERS ____ 17.
I believe it is okay for the mother to work once children are in elementary school.	*HIS ____ 18. HERS ____ 18.
I believe it is all right to call children names (e.g., dummy, stupid, idiot).	*HIS ____ 19. HERS ____ 19.
It is important to me that we have children as soon as possible.	*HIS ____ 20. HERS ____ 20.
I think it is important that we decide together when to start our family.	*HIS ____ 21. HERS ____ 21.
I believe both father and mother should be involved in the daily care of the children.	*HIS ____ 22. HERS ____ 22.
I think it is important for children to be involved in extra activities (e.g., dancing, sports, art and music lessons).	*HIS ____ 23. HERS ____ 23.
I am not sure I really want to have children.	*HIS ____ 24. HERS ____ 24.
I think reading to children is important.	*HIS ____ 25. HERS ____ 25.
I think it is important for children to know their parents love each other.	*HIS ____ 26. HERS ____ 26.
Children's behavior and manners are very important to me.	*HIS ____ 27. HERS ____ 27.
I think it is important for children to understand Christianity.	*HIS ____ 28. HERS ____ 28.
I believe it is very important for children to know that their parents love them.	*HIS ____ 29. HERS ____ 29.
I believe children should go to church even if they'd rather not.	*HIS ____ 30. HERS ____ 30.
I believe children should have their privacy respected.	*HIS ____ 31. HERS ____ 31.
I believe children should clean their plates.	*HIS ____ 32. HERS ____ 32.
I think it is the responsibility of the parents to teach children about sex and sexuality.	*HIS ____ 33. HERS ____ 33.

I plan to spank our children as a way of discipline.	*HIS ____ 34. HERS ____ 34.
I believe children should have chores and household jobs to do when they are old enough.	*HIS ____ 35. HERS ____ 35.
I think sons and daughters should be raised differently.	*HIS ____ 36. HERS ____ 36.
I believe it is okay for both parents to work.	*HIS ____ 37. HERS ____ 37.
I believe that larger families are better families.	*HIS ____ 38. HERS ____ 38.
I want our family to hold and hug each other.	*HIS ____ 39. HERS ____ 39.
I believe that only female children and women should set the table and wash dishes.	*HIS ____ 40. HERS ____ 40.
I believe that both the mother and the father should discipline the children.	*HIS ____ 41. HERS ____ 41.
I believe daily schedules are important for young children.	*HIS ____ 42. HERS ____ 42.
The number of children we have after marriage is important to me.	*HIS ____ 43. HERS ____ 43.
I believe children should be told and shown that their parents love them.	*HIS ____ 44. HERS ____ 44.
It is the parents' responsibility to help children with schoolwork.	*HIS ____ 45. HERS ____ 45.
The sex of our children is unimportant to me.	*HIS ____ 46. HERS ____ 46.
I believe it is all right to put off talking about children until after we are married.	*HIS ____ 47. HERS ____ 47.
I do not plan on having any children at all.	*HIS ____ 48. HERS ____ 48.
I would like to talk more about the possibility of birth defects in our children and how we would handle that.	*HIS ____ 49. HERS ____ 49.
I think we could be happy even if we found out we could not have children.	*HIS ____ 50. HERS ____ 50.

FAMILY PLANNING AND CHILDREN COMMUNICATION AND PERCEPTION EVALUATION

1. To evaluate the family planning and children section, compare your answers in both the "His" and "Hers" spaces from Worksheet I and give yourselves one point for each answer that is the same. There is a total of 50 points, two points for each statement. This is your communication and perception score for your families.

Family Communication and Perception Score _____

2. To evaluate the couple family planning and children section, compare your answers in both the "His" and "Hers" spaces from Worksheet II and give yourselves one point for each answer that is the same. There is a total of 100 points, two points for each statement. This is your communication and perception score as a couple.

Couple Communication and Perception Score _____

Total Family and Couple Communication and Perception Score _____

125–150 A score between 125 and 150 indicates that you have good communication and in many areas your perceptions are the same.

100–124 A score between 100 and 124 indicates that you may not have spent enough time together sharing your thoughts and feelings about yourselves and your families. Be open and honest with one another in these areas and set aside more time for serious talks.

0–99 If your score falls below 100, you still have much to learn about each other and your families. Communication is the key to a good relationship. You must begin sharing your thoughts and feelings in order to know how you agree and disagree.

In this evaluation, you have established the level of communication and perception you have in your relationship about family planning and children.

PROBLEM AREAS EVALUATION

To evaluate your problem areas or those areas requiring more attention, compare your answers in the following manner:

1. Take only the answers from the "*His" space on "His" Worksheet II and compare them to the answers from the "*Hers" space on "Her" Worksheet II. These are your answers about yourselves.

2. Compare these answers and give yourselves one point for each answer that is the same. There is a total of 50 points. This is your couple problem area score.

   Couple Problem Area Score _____

   40–50 A score between 40 and 50 indicates that you have some areas to discuss further but you are similar in most ways. Remember to seek a solution to your differences.

   0–39 A score of less than forty indicates that your backgrounds, your values, and your beliefs may not be compatible. You need to take more time to talk and, perhaps, to see a counselor before going on with marriage plans. Problem areas that are present before marriage will not just magically disappear after marriage.

Do not consider Worksheet I in the evaluation of problem areas for you as a couple.

FAMILY PLANNING AND CHILDREN COVENANT

Place your initials in the space following the responsibilities you agree to assume in the Family Planning and Children Covenant.

Marriage is a special kind of relationship. It is a covenant to be open, honest, faithful, and permanent. In our covenant concerning children and family planning we need to be very clear and honest about our feelings and thoughts. The conception of children is the one time mankind joins with God to be a part of the creation of a life. From love comes life.

1.	I agree that we may differ on many things, and I agree to respect your opinion and feelings.		
2.	I agree to be open and honest about my feelings and thoughts concerning children and family planning.		
3.	I agree that human life is a gift from God and will never abuse or destroy it.		
4.	I agree that we are answerable to God for the way we raise our children.		
5.	I agree that children should be raised, loved, and disciplined by both parents and I accept my responsibility in doing that.		
6.	I agree that, if for any reason, we come to a problem with children or birth control that we cannot solve, I will go with you to get professional help.		
7.	We have identified some statements about our relationship in family planning and children that we should take more time to discuss. I agree to set aside time to discuss with you the following: • _____ • _____ • _____ • _____ • _____		

I agree to this Covenant on Children and Family Planning because I love and respect you and want only the best for us in our marriage relationship.

Her signature: _____

I agree to this Covenant on Children and Family Planning because I love and respect you and want only the best for us in our marriage relationship.

His signature: _____

SUMMARY

As you and your spouse-to-be completed your work in this book, you probably have spent more time talking, sharing, learning, and growing together than many married couples do. It is our hope that you will use the knowledge you gained about yourselves, each other, and your families to strengthen your relationship and to set the stage for open, honest communication, respect for each other's differences, and creative problem solving in your marriage.

A good marriage relationship doesn't just happen. It requires commitment and dedication to the growth of each partner and to the growth of the relationship itself. A good marriage relationship takes work and time and energy. Let this be the beginning, not the end, of exploring your relationship and each other.

Remember, when you marry, you marry families!

JERRY D. HARDIN, MSMFT

Jerry D. Hardin has a bachelor of science degree in religion and philosophy from Friends University and a master of science degree in family studies and clinical family therapy from Friends University in Wichita, Kansas. Mr. Hardin served as a pastor over marriage and family life at Central Community Church and was founder and director of the Family Life Counseling Center. He served as a clinical marriage and family therapist, teacher, seminar speaker, and facilitator of marriage, family, and premarital workshops. He was a member of the American Association of Marriage and Family Therapists. Mr. Hardin served as a vocational consultant and president /CEO of Personnel Services, Inc. Jerry and his wife, Marilynn, have been married for more than fifty years and have three sons—Steve, Scott, and Paul—and seven grandchildren.

DIANNE C. SLOAN, MSMFT

Dianne C. Sloan has a bachelor of science degree in consumer sciences and family finance from Colorado State University and a masters of science degree from Friends University in Wichita, Kansas, in family studies and clinical family therapy. Ms. Sloan worked as a licensed clinical marriage and family therapist in private practice and educator for twenty-five years, retiring in 2012. In addition, Ms. Sloan provided clinical supervision for marriage and family graduate students at Friends University, postgraduate clinicians, and supervisors of supervision. She also served as a consultant and trainer for several agencies and churches in the Wichita area. From 1997 through 2001, Ms. Sloan worked for Kansas Children's Service League as the prevention/early intervention specialist, where she worked with KCSL Healthy Families, Head Start, and prevention programs statewide. Prior to 1997, Ms. Sloan was the director of the Center on Family Living, adjunct instructor with Friends University, and director of the Family Life Counseling Center at Central Community Church. Ms. Sloan is past president of the Kansas Association for Marriage and Family Therapy. She and her husband, Jim, have been married more than forty-five years and have one son, Jason, and two grandchildren.